THE GATEKEEPER

THE GATEKEEPER

A Novel

MICHAEL A. SISTI

Published by Orsini House

The Gatekeeper

ISBN Number 978-1-938-84232-0

Copyright © 2016 Michael A. Sisti
All Rights Reserved

No part of this book may be used or reproduced in any form or by any electronic or mechanical means, including information storage and retrieval systems, without permission in writing from the publisher.

Orsini House
Bradenton, FL 34201

Cover and text design by Michael A. Sisti
Layout consultant: Sara O. Sisti

All characters and events in this book are purely fictional, and any resemblance to persons living or dead, or actual events is purely coincidental.

This book is dedicated to all my friends
and family members who provided inspiration
for the personality composites used
in the development of the characters in this novel.

Acknowledgements

In order to create and embellish the many characters in this book, I appropriated names and name derivatives of people I know. I then blended many of the unique and fascinating personality traits from my huge circle of friends and my even larger extended family. And to that concoction, I added the fictitious negativity and evil actions the story required. I thank all of you for the use of select elements of your persona. And please accept as a compliment, my unauthorized utilization of those quirks that makes you so special.

Stephen Ackoury, "Your Mortgage CFO", with over 20 years' experience in banking, provided critical insights, edits and recommendations that influenced both the content and the format. He was particularly helpful with assistance on financial issues.

Chris Angermann, who edited my first novel, **Executive Crumple Zone**, gave me several key ideas about content, format and style. His advice, as always, was invaluable.

And I must thank my wife Sara, who tolerated my obsession to write this novel, and who read three successive iterations of the text, providing her insight, proofreading and typography skills.

This book is dedicated to all my friends
and family members who provided inspiration
for the personality composites used
in the development of the characters in this novel.

Part I

Building the Empire

Chapter 1

Shawn DiPisa rushed into the executive offices of Dizzy Don's, a discount appliance chain based in East Rutherford, New Jersey. Instead of going to Don Davino's office for his scheduled appointment, he went into the small, adjacent office occupied by Don's niece Dee Dee.

Even at 7:30 on a Monday morning, the chain's headquarters was bustling with action. There were a handful of sparsely appointed executive offices along the far wall, and most of the staff occupied paper-strewn desks in a central bullpen. And despite the activity, there seemed to be a businesslike discipline and an upbeat confidence that permeated the entire floor.

As he entered her office, Dee Dee smiled and said, "Shawn, thank you for meeting me on such short notice. I hated to call you at home this early, but I wanted to give you a heads-up on your eight o'clock meeting with my uncle. And please apologize to Laura for the early morning intrusion."

"Dee Dee, you never have to apologize for calling me at home. We've built our ad agency's business on strong customer service. Hell, I tell people I'm like a doctor, on call 24/7. Nowadays of course, that no longer applies to doctors. So what's the urgency?"

Donna (Dee Dee) Davino, is a thirty-something single, whose mother can't understand why no one has ever taken her hand in marriage.

Michael A. Sisti 3

She sees her daughter as voluptuous and Old World beautiful with dark penetrating eyes and wavy black hair. However, her beautiful face is overshadowed by a plus-sized body draped in frumpy clothes. With a more fashionable hairstyle and wardrobe, and the elimination of the extra-portion pasta dinners followed by the pastry desserts, she would be very attractive.

Dee Dee makes up for her appearance with a warm, engaging personality. She always gives you the comfort in knowing that she is there to help. And this nurturing characteristic makes her an invaluable asset at the family's retail appliance empire. Of course, she would like to be married, but her dedication to the job interferes with that goal. In addition, she doesn't put herself out there, partly because of her self-consciousness about her looks. But she also has a low esteem of her career achievements. She would like to have more decision-making responsibility instead of responding to her uncle and cousins' administrative needs.

In addition, Dee Dee's upbringing in an Italian Catholic family conflicts with her yearnings for intimacy. And her sensuousness, and mannerism of patting and touching people during conversation gives men the false sense that she is promiscuous. As a result, her experience with dating has always resulted in frustration and disappointment. Dee Dee would prefer men to appreciate her as a loving person rather than a big-busted sex object. Her expectation is to be romanced by her suitors, rather than be groped and fondled on a first date.

"Shawn, Uncle Don is going to ask you for a big favor this morning. As you know, he recently hired his shit-for-brains son-in-law Whitney and has decided to make him the marketing director."

Shocked by this revelation, Shawn blurted out, "What is he thinking? And what about Donny, junior? He's been handling the marketing since we started. Whitney really doesn't have a clue about marketing. How can he possibly manage a multi-million-dollar budget? Is Don really going to trust him to handle that much money?

"The simple answer is, he trusts you. You're going to have to become both the client and the account executive in the short term. And at the same time, you will have to teach him everything you know about advertising and marketing."

Shawn was incredulous with this poorly conceived plan. "Hold on. What's the rush? Why doesn't Whit go back to school and study marketing? And here's an even better idea. He could take night courses and work at my agency during the day, assuming Don will keep him on your firm's payroll. That would cut the learning curve in half."

"For the average person, that would be a good solution. But we're talking about Whit, so let's be serious. He has this superiority complex, thinking that he already possesses all the knowledge that any college can deliver. And quite frankly, he will never learn enough to truly take over the marketing for the company. Your challenge will be to navigate this minefield. Shawn, you're going to have to manage both sides of this process, try to feed some knowledge into his dormant brain, and keep him from screwing up. Going forward, this will be your new description of customer service around here."

At that point, a smiling Don Davino poked his head into Dee Dee's office and said to Shawn, "I see my niece has already told you my plan. Come down to my office and let's go over the details. Shawn, I really want this to work out, and I'm counting on you to make it happen."

Don, who has a deep respect for Shawn, and while seated behind his large, orderly desk, directed him to teach Whit everything possible about the marketing business, and to make absolutely sure that Whit did not make any detrimental moves or wrong decisions.

Don also explained that his son Donny would now take over acquiring new properties as the chain planned to rapidly expand its locations.

Once Don felt that Shawn understood his added duties, he brought him down to Whit's office and outlined the new ground rules. Then Don left Whit's office so two men could have an informal discussion about the indoctrination to the chain's marketing effort. Shawn quickly recognized that Whitney, while apprehensive about his new responsibility was excited about the new position. He had a disarming smile and gave people the impression that he was always having fun. He was athletically built, having played tennis in college, and he still dressed like he was on campus.

Chapter

2

As Shawn came off the elevator at his agency's office, he greeted his secretary, "Good morning, Deb. Please assemble the creative team into the conference room right away."

Debbie Russo responded, "You mean the entire staff, don't you?" This was more of a statement than a question. His response to her was a smile and a wink.

Shawn's self-described Broken Brooklynese accent immediately gave away his origins, although he dressed far differently than the residents from that infamous borough. His one fashion trademark was his loud Jerry Garcia ties, which contrasted his conservative Italian suits. Shawn's brown eyes had permanent smile wrinkles around them and his thin lips were set in a constant smirk.

Shawn's philosophy when he founded the small advertising agency three years ago was that everyone has the ability to think creatively and develop innovative ideas. And so, all eighteen employees at Image Concepts were part of the creative team. He expected each of them to participate in the brainstorming sessions and he encouraged them to contribute their suggestions, whether they proved to be good, mediocre or just plain awful. He often said that there are no bad ideas, because even an idea that isn't appropriate may trigger a better one from another team member. So when he had the space built out in their office building, he requested that the conference room take up nearly a quarter of the entire floor plan. Like the rest of the office space on the top floor of the three-story contemporary building they occupied, it was open and bright with an abundance of windows. The walls throughout the floor were decorated with examples of their work and the hundreds of awards they accumulated. As you entered these offices, you immediately recognized the creativity and joy that permeated the space. Clients and vendors always looked forward to visiting Image Concepts, and some actually hinted that they were interested in working for the company.

Shawn and his wife Laura launched the firm with the encouragement of one of his freelance clients. He was a creative thinking entrepreneur who thrived on motivating consumers through innovative marketing communications. He and Laura, his wife of 10 years had one of those rare marriages that allowed them to live, work and even play golf together, constantly enjoying each other's company.

He met Laura at Ramapo College where he was studying graphic design in a two-year associate degree program. Laura was a four-year bachelor student earning a communications degree in Media. He was introduced to her by one of his classmates, and became immediately smitten. He was taken by her beautiful hazel eyes, and couldn't stop staring at her. Recognizing that he was making her nervous, Shawn invited her for coffee after class that day and there was instant chemistry. Since neither of them was in a serious relationship, he asked her out on Valentine's Day the following week.

In preparation for the date, Shawn went to a florist to buy a dozen red roses, but was shocked at the price the florists charged on this holiday. So instead he bought one long-stem rose. He then went to the art supply store and bought poster board and a roll of white craft paper. With these materials and his marking pens he created a huge 18x24 greeting card with the rose taped to the front, and wrapped it in an envelope he made from the paper. Shawn presented it to her at the restaurant, causing a commotion, as everyone wanted to see what was in the huge envelope. His creativity proved to be more effective than any bouquet of roses. And it locked in a relationship that would last a lifetime.

When Shawn graduated, he immediately got a job with Blue Cross Blue Shield in their marketing department. He and Laura continued to date while she completed her degree program, and following that, he wanted to get married. Laura put him off, saying that she was not ready for marriage. About a year before she got out of school, Blue Cross offered Shawn an opportunity to complete his bachelor's program with night classes at the company's expense. During this time, he told Laura that as soon as he got his degree, they were going to get married, so she should start making plans for the wedding.

Laura was only five feet tall, with thick auburn hair. Her beautiful eyes were set in an oval face. She had a trim, toned body that was the result of an active sports life including hiking, tennis, golf and skiing. She loved people, and her penchant for inclusion always made everyone feel totally comfortable in her company.

When the staff was gathered together in the large conference room, Shawn announced the major change at the agency's largest client, Dizzy Don's. "Early this morning, Don's secretary, Dee Dee called me at home. She requested that I come to their office first thing for an important eight AM meeting with Don Davino. She also asked that I meet with her for coffee beforehand to give me a heads-up on Don's reorganization plan. His new son-in-law, Whitney Cogswell joined the retailer recently, and will now be taking over all of the advertising and marketing responsibilities. Effective immediately, he will replace Donny Jr. who will concentrate full time on opening up new locations. And going forward we will be working with Whit on a daily basis to plan and run all their advertising and other marketing activities. She also warned me that he has zero experience in marketing."

At that point Laura interjected, "Now, aren't you glad you listened to me and gave Whitney and Lucille that extra special wedding present."

"Yes, it was an excellent idea. And I always listen to you." With that exchange, smiles went around the room. Everyone knew that Shawn ran the agency, and Laura ran Shawn.

Shawn then explained to the staff that Lucille was Lucille Davino, Don's only daughter who had married Whitney Cogswell IV. He went on to say that after his early morning meeting with Dee Dee, he met with Don who gave him all the details about the restructure. And he further explained that the purpose of this appointment was to create a meaningful position for Whitney within the family's retail organization.

Shortly before his daughter's wedding, Don had offered Whit a job with the company. He thought this would be the only way to assure that his daughter would continue to enjoy her affluent lifestyle. Whit had been in a dead-end job as an entry-level executive at a manufacturing company, and had no management skills. He exhibited no drive to succeed, but expected to land in a position of wealth without doing any heavy lifting.

Don had also learned that Whit's family was broke, despite their appearance of a high society, country club lifestyle. Don was confident that if he put Whit in marketing, he couldn't cause too much damage. Of course, Shawn, recognizing the importance of marketing questioned Don on the decision. And Don had responded, "I'm comfortable with the decision, because I know you won't let Whitney make any costly mistakes."

As Shawn recounted the morning with his staff, he warned them, "Don't initiate any directive from Whit without my approval. Until he gets settled in this new position and understands how the process works, he is going to want to change everything. Going forward, he will want all the advertising to have his stamp on it rather than Donny Junior's. So we have to create a new campaign for the next grand opening."

Laura jumped in, "Why do we need a new campaign? We've done so many of these now that we have a formula. And that's the way they like it. It's a good program, and we don't have to reinvent the wheel every time, plus they save money."

Shawn responded with the quote he usually reserves for when clients or visitors attended the creative sessions. "Keep in mind that I'm one of the 20 smartest people in this room." Everyone laughed. Laura sighed.

Continuing, he said, "I have already thought about the solution. We are not going to start from scratch. We're just going to make some design modifications to the layout, and Whit can call it his own. This is the first job where he has any responsibility, and the ego factor will be kicking in immediately. And it will be my task, among so many others, to keep it under control."

After a brief discussion of some layout ideas, the meeting broke up, and Laura followed Shawn into his office. "Shawn, how do you think this is going to affect the account, long term? You know how concerned I am about them. Except for Don himself, no one in the family has the ability to run a company that size. Dee Dee told me that her cousin Lucille married Whitney because, coming from a Waspy family, he seems so much classier than her two brothers. But apparently he's a spoiled kid and he doesn't have much in the brains department. What if he tries to make an impression on the Davino family and decides to bring in a new ad agency?"

"Laura, Don is a street-smart, self-made son of an immigrant. He recognizes a good work ethic. While his two sons are devoted, they don't have the skill set to run a customer-focused retail business. And there aren't any other family members in the business that could ever take over. But he appreciates that I understand his business and how to market it. He values how hard I work for him. And he knows that out of loyalty to him, I turned down the Two Wyse Guys account, which is a client with a much larger budget, and his biggest competitor.

"There's no question that it's dangerous having so much of our profit coming from one customer, but it's hard to find the time to call on any new prospects. I agree that we must get more clients to balance out the ratio. Whit is going to be high maintenance, leaving me with even less time to chase business. At least with Donny, he left me alone to run the advertising. Maybe we should try again to hire a sales executive."

"I agree that we've got to do something, but we've had so many bad experiences with sales reps. They all have cost us money without bringing in a dime's worth of business. Look at that guy Mel you hired. He drew tens of thousands of dollars against zero commissions, didn't crack one account, and then sued us when you fired him. And adding insult to injury, the judge awarded him even more money. If we ever hire another account executive, I will conduct the interviews. You just don't have that intuition gene that we women have. I can see right through these phonies, while you think they all have potential leaking out of their eyes.

"Shawn, if we ever lose Dizzy Don's before we get some new accounts, we're out of business. It's that simple."

But Shawn never worried about losing his big account, or about failure of any kind. After leaving Blue Cross, he had always been able to make a comfortable living as a freelance creative director or production consultant, despite Laura's concern for his lack of a steady paycheck.

Shawn got a big break when a dramatic, award-winning billboard campaign he produced for an auto dealer was written up in the area's business weekly newspaper. The story prompted Don Davino to call Shawn and give him a design project. Even with the more than 30-year age difference, the two men hit it off right from the beginning. When the project's results far exceeded expectations, Don offered to help Shawn launch his own ad agency. And so, Shawn handling the creative and account service tasks, with Laura running the administration and production, they set out on their own. In three years the agency grew with the addition of some small accounts, but Dizzy Dons represented the bulk of the income and the sole reason for their fast-paced growth.

Chapter

3

"Get Serena McCormack on the phone," barked Ben Rusk to his assistant, Elaine Thompson. Ben is the Chairman and CEO of Ramapo Interbank, a small bank holding company, which he is trying to grow through acquisition. Ben is aggressive, gruff and often hostile in his takeover attempts, but he hasn't lost a deal on his terms yet. Even outside the office, he's a hard-charging, dominant presence, who prefers squash to racket ball, and likes a Cohiba cigar with his Laphroaig 25 single malt scotch.

"Serena, it's Ben. Are we going to get this deal completed by the end of the month? If not, I'm moving on."

Serena McCormack is the CEO of Catskill Bank & Trust. She is an attractive woman with dark red curly hair and the most beautiful green eyes that are almost too large for her face. Her self-assured style and classic Irish good looks caught the attention of Catskill's founder, who accelerated her career from bank teller to CEO in less than five years. However, it took a lot more than a pretty face to succeed in the male-dominated business of banking. McCormack was tough as nails, and stood up to anyone who threatened her success. When pushed, she dropped the feminine charm and battled like one of the guys.

"Ben, I don't see how this acquisition will ever happen. You have reneged on every single term we agreed on. You have cut the share price by $10, which my board will never accept. You have reduced my personal contract to three years, and your plan to terminate every other officer of this bank has my board members furious. Get back to the terms of the original letter of intent, and we can get this done. Otherwise, it's over."

"Look Serena, I'm not going to play games with you. Our due diligence report shows that your capitalization is far lower that you stated at the outset, and your losses are projecting higher. How can I hold to the original terms?"

"I'm sending you an email right now. You read it and decide if the deal is dead." With that, Ben abruptly hung up and pressed *Send* on his computer. The email addressed to Serena McCormack at Catskill Bank contained no text, but an attachment that read:

Media Communiqué
For Release on March 21, 2003

Ramapo Interpublic Denies Merger Plans with Catskill Regional Bank

In an effort to dispel rumors regarding a merger between Ramapo Interpublic and Catskill Bank & Trust, Ben Rusk, Chairman and CEO confirmed that his bank holding company has no plans to acquire CB&T.

Rusk explained, "Although we conducted some due diligence of this bank among so many others, we have been unable to find common ground, and have declined this opportunity on behalf of our shareholders."

Ramapo Interpublic enjoys a flawless reputation for growth and value for its shareholders. This is the result of astute management of its assets, plus carefully selected merger and acquisition partners. Our selection process always avoids potential candidates with troubled histories.

Over the last four years, this banking institution has more than

doubled in size, and its share price has nearly tripled.
Direct all inquiries to BRUSK@RamapoInterpublic.com.

Within minutes, Elaine Thompson was on the intercom telling Ben that, as expected, Serena McCormack was back on the line.

"Ben, you can't pull this bullshit on me. This is nothing more than a veiled blackmail threat. It is absolutely unethical. The release implies that we are a flawed acquisition prospect. And that will certainly hurt our image. If this gets into the press, I will have our attorney file a defamation suit against you, and expose your predatory practices to the regulators. I will see that you never get the opportunity to acquire another bank again. I can't believe we even considered selling to an asshole like you."

"Calm down Serena, and listen to me. First of all, we are already a regional banking force and on our way to become one of the largest in the Greater New York area. I count the President of the United States among my friends. Now do you actually think the banking commission is going to accept the claims of a hysterical CEO of a backwater bank struggling to survive, against Ben Rusk? Would you like me to share my observations of your management staff and your finances with the regulators? Even your trust officer has been negligent by not performing an audit on your trust clients' life insurance policies.

'Now, here's what we're going to do. You go back to your board and get them to accept my deal. We will sweeten the offer by two dollars a share, and we will extend your personal services contract to five years, with a $50,000 salary increase, plus a guaranteed bonus. We will keep all your officers in place for at least one year. If you and they prove their mettle, you can earn permanent status. This offer is on the table until Monday. I want the deal to close before the end of the quarter."

"You sure don't leave me much choice. I'll call an emergency board meeting. And Ben, I can't imagine working for you more than five years. You are a ruthless bastard!"

"Yes, but a benevolent one as you will find out. You will be glad to be on my team. I take very good care of my people."

Following the phone call, Ben walked out to the small balcony off his office and enjoyed the view of the Ramapo Mountains that stretched out before him. His lavishly furnished and expansive office was on the top floor of a building in Mahwah, NJ with beautiful views north and east. He sat on a lounge chair, lit up a cigar, and relaxed for a few minutes, savoring the win he just achieved, and the serenity of his perch.

He was proud of his toughness that he always tempered with generous compensation for those who were hardworking and loyal to him. He grew up as an only child in a poor family. His father was a weak, spineless person who never asserted himself, but rather kept a low profile at the office where he worked as an accounting clerk. As a result, he was always passed over for promotion. His mother would have liked to get a job to help support the family, but her husband's pride never allowed it. Instead, she kept an immaculate, albeit sparsely furnished home and focused her energy on raising her son. And despite being a difficult taskmaster, she rewarded him with little gifts for his achievements in school.

As a teenager, Ben began to earn money for himself by working odd jobs and saving every penny in a cigar box at home. Fascinated by the cash, he would periodically walk several blocks to the bank just to exchange his loose change and wrinkled bills for newly printed currency. During his high school years, Ben began lending money to his friends and charging them small interest fees. And when the loans were due, he insisted on being repaid in new dollar bills.

By the time he got to college, Ben Rusk had organized an informal loan company that he operated out of his dorm room at Rutgers. He started out making small loans to his classmates, even cashing paychecks from their part time employment. And soon he was providing funds to both students and faculty throughout the vast campus in New Brunswick.

His earnings were such that he was able to fund the education costs that were not covered by his partial scholarship, plus enough to pay for his MBA at Wharton School in Philadelphia.

After his graduation, Ben went to work for a small bank in Ramsey. He almost immediately recognized that the owner had no clue about making money in the banking business. He also realized that his employer had lost interest in being a banker. So after only two years, Ben was able to strike a deal to acquire the bank in a leveraged buyout pact. And from that obscure beginning, he launched his dream to build a major banking enterprise.

Chapter

Dee Dee stood in the doorway of Don Davino's office, waiting for him to hang up his phone and invite her in. "Uncle Don, your plan for Whitney is just not working. He really doesn't fit in. He's nothing more than a pretentious fool, thinking he can snap his fingers at me and make things happen. The real problem is that he has been spoiled his entire life by his pompous WASP family. Look how we were treated at their country club in Connecticut during the wedding. They are up to their ass in hock, trying to keep up appearances in their snooty Darien neighborhood. And it's probably because of that kind of upbringing, that he has no sense of reality.

"And your son Donny is not happy about giving up the marketing. He's questioning every move Whitney makes. Isn't he supposed to be just in charge of real estate now?"

Don Davino sat at his desk, exasperated that he had to deal with problems such as this. He had built a very successful retail business by using his talent to talk to people in a disarming way so that they immediately trusted him.

When training new employees, Don liked to tell the story of when he was a young boy living in a tenement in lower Manhattan. Their widowed neighbor bought a stove from a merchant who sold used furniture and appliances from his truck that he drove around the area. After collecting the money for the stove, the merchant left it on the sidewalk and drove off. Don's father and a couple of men from the building came to the frantic woman's assistance and carried the stove up to her apartment. Don watched his father install it, only to realize the stove didn't work. He then set about to repair it, and get it functioning properly.

The lessons Don learned that day stayed with him and guided his career. Always respect your customer. If you sell them something, then give them more than they expect. Sell only premium merchandise. Always be honest, and confront their issues head on.

With that in mind, he responded, "Okay Dee Dee, I'll talk to Donny again, but it's going to be up to you to get between your cousin and Whit. You're the only one around here that can get it done because everyone loves you. And that can't be said about most other people in this company. He won't get upset with you, and that will diffuse the situation until Whit comes into his own. I made you Whit's assistant for one important reason. It will be your job to protect him and make him productive. Use your brains, and influence Whit's decisions so he doesn't mess up. Come to me only if you have to, but you should be able to handle it on your own. And use Shawn to keep coaching him and pushing him into the right decisions. In the meantime, as we move forward, Donny will be out of the office most days, meeting with real estate brokers, and scouting locations for new stores."

"Uncle Don, people like me because I tell it like it is, and I have a way of doing it without offending them. And now I've got to say some things to you. So don't be upset.

"Take a look at where you are. You started out in a rented storefront selling used appliances and stuff, and you were successful because you understand people. Now you have 30 major discount stores, and you own all the buildings and the land under them. You are also planning to double the number of stores in the next few years. You're not getting any younger, so who is going to take over this business? You've got two sons that could never handle it. Donny has no people skills, but I will say that he does have a set of balls." Don interrupted, "Dee Dee, talk polite."

"Sorry, Uncle Don. But I'm right. He really doesn't have the personality or the temperament to take over. And Angelo, even though he runs Facilities Maintenance, is nothing more than Junior's shadow. He follows him around like a puppy dog."

"Dee Dee, don't underestimate Donny. He's really got a knack for finding the best locations, and negotiating good real estate deals. It's just that when he opens his mouth, he sounds like a fuckin' *stunade*."

Smiling, Dee Dee responded, "Uncle Don, talk polite. But seriously, Donny can run the real estate, but he can't run the business. And now you've got Whitney in the organization, and you yourself admit that he'll never be able to take over. He can't find the zipper to his fly. You have got to start planning for a management succession. If for no other reason, think of the family. Besides, at this point you should be thinking about enjoying your money and not dealing with the daily hassles of running a retail empire."

"I've thought about retiring, but what am I gonna do, sit around with all your aunts? I need the *vig*. I need the juice that I get from running this place. I'm just not ready to give it up. And don't worry your pretty little head. This company will be around for a long time and so will I."

Chapter

5

At seven in the morning, Shawn and Whit sat at a table near the back of the Suburban Diner on Route 17. Even at this hour the chrome and vinyl icon was bustling with customers, and wait staff rushing around pouring coffee.

"Whitney, thank you for agreeing to meet with me regularly for breakfast. I can't tell you how much I appreciate your willingness to learn this new discipline. And I know it will really expedite your ability to manage the marketing process. I am confident that you will grow into this position and be very successful."

"No. Thank you Shawn for offering to take the time out of your busy day. I agree this is going to help me personally, and I really appreciate it. I think this indoctrination effort will go quickly. I don't see advertising, or marketing as you call it, being all that complicated. You decide what products you want to put on sale next week, run some ads and people rush to your stores. It's easy because everybody loves a bargain."

"Well OK, but it's a little more complicated than that. We'd better start with the basics. First of all, effective marketing is not about offering products at bargain prices. You have to start by building a brand. In our case it's based on value and integrity. Do you have any idea how many discount store chains in the New York area have gone out of business in the last 50 years, all trying to be the low-price leader?"

Shawn went on to explain that advertising is an investment where you look to get the maximum return on the amount you spend. This is achieved by making the communications effective and enhancing the brand image.

Toward the end of the meeting, he went on to advise Whit on what to expect in the near future. "Over the next few months, as your appointment of Director of Marketing gets publicized, every ad agency in the metropolitan area will be hammering on your door to pitch your account. And they are going to tell you about the great advertising they do. But it's not really about the advertising. It's about the brand.

"When I got out of college, I worked at Blue Cross and learned about the power of branding. People were willing to pay a higher premium because it was Blue Cross insurance.

"So when I run an ad campaign for Dizzy Don's, I'm not selling an underpriced refrigerator, I'm selling the value of the store chain. Your main competitor, Two Wyse Guys, despite being a smaller chain than you, runs twice as much advertising as you do, with ads screaming low price. And they do well, as long as their prices are actually the lowest. But you can't always be the bottom feeder. Sooner or later you're going to burn out. Their profit margins are much lower than yours.

"It's like the used car dealer who boasts that he loses a thousand dollars on every sale. When asked how he stays in business, he answers, 'Volume!'"

"Getting back to the marketing. We make sure that we exceed our customer's expectations when they buy from Dizzy Don's. I even go out into the field and train the staff in each store on their role in the branding process."

"I guess there really is more to this process than I would have expected. I'm still confident that it will come to me quickly. But I'm not convinced about the price issue. People always go for the low price."

"You'll get to see how that works soon enough. If you're willing to meet with me regularly, you'll know as much as I do in no time. But that's enough for today. Let's go to work. We'll get together again next Monday. In the meantime, call me with any questions you have."

Chapter 6

That evening Whit and Lucille sat in the living room of their sparsely furnished, high-rise apartment on Palisade Avenue in Fort Lee. Whit was on his second martini, while Lucille sipped red wine. He was sharing the highlights of his breakfast meeting with Shawn. "I will tell you, Lucille, I am completely impressed with the effort Shawn is taking to help bring me up to speed on the marketing process. He sincerely wants me to be successful, and I have to admire that. My only criticism is that he makes more about this marketing effort than is there. It is not really that complicated. And I think I have most of it already figured out. After all, I am intelligent and a quick learner. And I do have a business degree from UConn."

"Whitney, don't think you know it all. My father's success owes a lot to the way Shawn's company manages his marketing. Sales really started accelerating when his company came on board. So you need to pay attention to everything he says, and respect his recommendations."

"I intend to learn everything he has to offer. And then I'll make the decisions. Some of Shawn's thinking, especially about sale pricing is flawed. But I've got bigger plans than marketing. Your father will want to retire in a few years, and I'll be the guy to step in and take over."

"Don't get ahead of yourself, Whitney. My father has been in this business for 30 years, and he didn't learn it overnight. But I do admire your ambition."

"Listen, Lucy. I am not waiting 30 years to run this company. I am ready to start moving ahead now. And speaking of moving, I have been looking at a new Lamborghini that I want to lease. It is a car that truly makes a statement."

With that Lucille jumped off the couch, nearly spilling her wine. "What! Are you crazy? We can barely afford this apartment that you insisted we rent, and we haven't even furnished it yet. And you want to get a Lamborghini? You park a car like that in the company lot and my father will fire you."

Chapter

7

Dee Dee had been at her desk since 7:30, when at about eight o'clock the phone rang. "Mr. Cogswell's office, this is Dee Dee. How may I help you?"

"Good morning. Can I speak to him?"

"I'm sorry, but he doesn't get in until nine. Is there something I can help you with?"

"Well, I was hoping to get him before his day started. This is Fred Krump from the Krump Agency. I have some ideas for advertising that I wanted to discuss with him. Can you have him call me?"

"Mr. Krump, I can tell you we have no plans to change agencies at this time. Why don't you send me some information on your agency, and I will keep it on file for Mr. Cogswell. We've been getting lots of calls from agencies since the announcement of his appointment. So I have set up a file of interested ad agencies for future reference."

"That's all well and good, but I have some important information that he will want to hear about right away. Can you set up just a brief appointment for me to see him?"

"That just won't be possible. He is far too busy to see prospective agencies at this time. But as I said, send me your information. Bye now."

As she completed the call, a stranger wearing a business suit and carrying a briefcase, walked up to her desk and said, "Hi. There was no one at the front desk, so I walked back here. I am Roger Farnsworth, a former classmate of Whit from UConn. Can I see him?"

"Sorry Mr. Farnsworth, but he isn't in yet, and he doesn't see anyone without an appointment. What's this in reference to?"

"I am with the Fairfield Agency in Connecticut and I want to talk to him about his advertising."

"I can tell you that we have no plans to change agencies, but why don't you leave me some of your information and I'll see that it gets into our reference file in the event we want to choose another agency."

"Here is my card and my presentation kit. Please be sure to give it to him. He will definitely want to talk to me. And tell him, if he does not get back to me, I will follow up with a call to him."

"I'll be glad to do that. And you have a good day."

When Farnsworth left, Dee Dee tossed his material in the trash, along with all of the other ad agency brochures and flyers that were coming in the mail almost daily.

Chapter

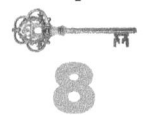

"Hi Shawn, this is Whitney. I wanted to talk to you about the radio advertising."

"Sure Whit, what's up?"

"I am really not happy with the current flight. It is totally boring and no one is listening to the commercials. I happen to be looking for a car, so I have been following the auto dealer ads. And they are full of energy. You cannot help but pay attention to them. We need to make people stop and listen. Our announcer needs to raise the volume and shout out a deal that makes people want to buy the appliances we have on sale."

"Actually, Whit, that's not a good tactic. Dizzy Don's sells premium brands with value pricing, and of course, we always include a loss leader or two. Our customer profile is the quality-conscious consumer who wants to feel assured that they bought a superior product at a good price, and it will be supported for the life of the product with excellent customer service. They don't ever want us to insult their intelligence with an outrageous offer by someone yelling at them through a radio speaker. What you're describing is the Two Wyse Guys ads, and we always want to distinguish ourselves from them. So think about it and you'll see that we made the right decision on the style and tone of the advertising we do. Having said that, Whit, don't ever hesitate to bring me your ideas, as I never want to discourage you. Our collaboration is important."

After Shawn hung up, Whit called in Dee Dee and began to vent to her. "Now that I am really understanding the marketing, I am concluding that Shawn's work is not that terrific. In fact, it is the same stuff over and over. I just came up with a much better way for our radio advertising to really break through, and Shawn shot it down. Who does he think he is? I am the Director of Marketing."

"Slow down Whitney. I hate to say this, but your knowledge of marketing fits in Shawn's pinkie. You know just enough to be dangerous, but not enough to give direction or make decisions. He is a student of the profession and one of the best branding experts around. You, on the other hand, don't know what you don't know. And if you look at our sales over the years, and the corresponding profit, you will see that after we hired Image Concepts, our sales really began to climb, and our profits right along with them. We are one of the most successful independent retailers in the New York area. And it was Shawn's direction that made it all happen."

"Oh, that is nonsense. Our growth mirrors the economy's growth, and it is certainly not because of anything Shawn did. His work is very dated and not at all exciting. And very soon I'm going to make some major changes and put some noise and excitement in our advertising. I may even put myself in the commercials and become the spokesman for the company. I know how to deliver the message that people want to hear."

"Stop it, Whitney. My role in this company is to protect you and make you successful. You have very big plans for yourself, and if you want to achieve them you had better listen to me. I'm sorry to say it, but right now you sound like a fool. There aren't many places in this company where you can be productive. So if you screw up in Marketing, you could wind up in the warehouse, jockeying washing machines with a forklift. And with the thinking you just described, that is exactly what will happen.

"Your success relies on Shawn and on me. And don't ever forget it."

Although effectively chastised, Cogswell was not convinced, and he was still seething that both Shawn and Dee Dee were overruling him. But his time will come. And it will be soon.

Chapter  9

The atmosphere at the hastily called board meeting of the Morristown National Bank was similar to the moments just before an electrical storm. It was quiet and tense. The room was warm and humid, as if the air conditioning was turned off. Sitting there, you could feel the static and smell the ozone.

Tom Mitchell, the bank's CEO stood up and began to pace before he addressed the group. He was tall with constantly tousled dark hair that emphasized his boyish good looks, but belied a very deliberate demeanor. Tom took nothing at face value, and questioned the motives of anyone trying to influence him or sell him something. His was a personality that bordered on paranoia. But that happened to be an important characteristic for a bank president, with decisions that most often leaned very conservative.

"Fellow Board Members, let me tell you why I called this emergency meeting. And before we start, understand that there will be no minutes taken. In fact, this meeting never took place.

"Last year, we entered the largest real estate deal in the history of the bank with one of our key clients, Tafik Husani. Most of you know of Mr. Husani and are aware that over the past few years, we have successfully transacted many deals where his loans were all repaid well before maturity.

"In a very convoluted series of transactions, Husani borrowed a total of $47.8 million for the acquisition of several parcels on the Navesink River in Monmouth County. He was preparing to flip the parcels to a developer for a huge mixed-use residential and commercial development. He, in fact, already owned one of the smaller parcels outright. Everything was in order, including the sales history of the properties and the appraisals he provided. The land in question was considered to be in a recession-proof area of the state, and as you all know his track record was flawless. Also it goes without saying, our attorney reviewed the contract he had with the developer, so we allowed the deal to flow smoothly.

"I personally attended the series of closings at Husani's lawyer's office, that took nearly all day to complete. And in the end, I called in the wire transfers.

"Last month Mr. Husani missed an interest payment, the second on the loan, which calls for a balloon by the end of this year, when the final transfer of title takes place with the developer.

"When my calls to Husani went unanswered, I called his lawyer who told me that he has had no contact from Husani since the closing a few months back. I then tried to locate the developer, and it turns out that the company doesn't even exist.

"At the same time, I had my assistant Ruth track down some of the sellers of the parcels that were purchased through this deal. Most of them turned out to be shell companies with origins in the Middle East. Apparently these parcels were sold back and forth, sometimes twice on the same day, for rapidly escalating amounts. Each transaction geometrically increased the appraised value of all the lots, inflating them way beyond true market value.

"Since Ruth's brother lives in the area, she asked him to drive out and actually take a look at the physical properties. He claims that from what he can tell, it is mostly wetlands and tidal dunes, nothing you could ever build on.

"Ladies and gentlemen, I am sorry to say that we may very well be out nearly $50 million."

Among the immediate buzz, the chairman was the first to speak. "Tom, I can't believe you could allow this to happen. As the custodian of the bank's assets, you are the perfect personality for the role. Simply put, you just don't trust people. How did Husani put this over on you?"

"I will admit that I dropped my guard. He is a charming individual, always showering us with little thoughtful gifts. And his history with us has been absolutely impeccable. We all passed on this deal, and no one voiced a single objection. When we calculated the profit, our greed obviously clouded our judgment. And for these reasons, we probably didn't review all the documentation carefully enough.

"But right now we can't dwell on how we let it happen. Later we can go back and re-examine the process. We are faced with a survival issue of monumental proportions. With a loss like this on the books, the bank examiners will shut us down in a minute. We've got to find an angel investor or sell the bank. And we're all going to take a huge hit on our personal investments in the bank."

"Tom, do you have any candidates for an acquisition?" The question came from Joanne Buning, the bank's largest investor.

"As you know, Ben Rusk keeps calling me, offering to merge us into his holding company. He claims that every bank and its investors has done better over the long-term, following a merger with him, even in a distressed situation.

"I am planning to talk to Ben following this meeting, and I will also quietly shop us around. But we have to move quickly, before this problem loan goes into default. And before I call in the FBI."

Chapter 10

"Donny was sitting in his office, having coffee with Angelo and scanning the morning paper when he saw the new Dizzy Don's ad. Enraged, he tossed the paper to his brother and shouted, "Lookit this shit. They changed the fuckin' ads."

He immediately dialed Whit's office and said, "Dee Dee, I need to speak to the asshole. Why did he change the ads? I worked my balls off to get them just right."

"Dominic, his name is Whitney, and he's your brother-in-law, not an asshole. He worked out the new design with Shawn, and everybody likes it. Besides, this isn't your department anymore. And when are you going to learn to talk like a businessman, and not like a *cafone*?"

"Lookit Dee Dee, don't fuck with my head. I have no problem makin' myself understood. Not like Mr. Whitney, the Fuckin' Fourth, Cogswell with that phony accent that makes him sound like he's got a two by four stuck up his ass. Now, put Dickhead on the phone."

"Whitney is in a meeting and he will have to call you back. And his accent is a cultured New England parlance that you will never be able to achieve. But don't hang up. I want you to listen to me, it's important. There's a good possibility that you are going to be running this entire operation someday. And starting now, you'll be negotiating very large real estate deals with sophisticated businessmen and realtors. It's not like when you were a kid. You can't solve problems with your fists and your foul mouth. You've got to earn everyone's respect. In order to do that, you have to clean up your image. Underneath all that grunge is a good-looking guy. Get rid of the 'stash and the scruffy shadow, start dressing better, you can afford it. And take a class in public speaking. Learn to talk like an educated American. If you look and act the part of a successful executive, you'll control the situation and then you can get anything you want. Think about it and you'll see that I'm right."

"If you're such a fuckin' expert on fashion, why don't you fix yourself up and get a husband."

Dee Dee flinched, as the comment really hurt her, and she had all to do to keep from hanging up on her cousin, but she recovered and said, "The new ad design was Shawn's decision, so talk to him if you have to. He can explain why we made the change. But remember that it isn't your marketing department anymore." And she quickly disconnected the call.

Chapter 11

"Bobby, what's going on? It's getting to be time to make our move."

Ben Rusk was calling C. Robert "Bobby" Willis on his cell phone. Bobby was in his corner office at Mid-Atlantic Trust, a position attained through his opportunistic and cunning mindset despite his lack of management skills. He overcame his dearth of leadership ability through manipulation and bluster. Until he met Ben, his career had consisted of a succession of middle management positions at several banks. He never got to the executive suite because his impatience drove him to avoid hard work and find every shortcut. Ben recognized Bobby's character fault and his "end justifies the means" attitude that he felt he could exploit.

Before responding to Ben, Bobby waved his assistant, Marianne Clark out of the office. "Hi Ben. I agree. I think we're ready to deal. Your plan was brilliant and everything has fallen into place, just as you envisioned. First, I never thought that you could convince John Youngman to bring me in as CEO. His ego is a mile wide, which is probably why the bank is in so much trouble. And you were right. Suggesting that he become board chairman guaranteed that nothing would change for the better. I've had no problem expanding our retail base. In two years, we've opened 17 new branch offices all over the state. The way you seeded the first few offices with depositors and commercial accounts, actually encouraged Youngman to expand at an even faster rate. He had no idea that you were providing the people that were the new customers opening those accounts. And now that those bogus customers are closing their accounts in droves, we're overextended and facing a severe shortfall in capital.

"We will have an interim board report by the end of the week. You should call Youngman next week for a little chat. He's really nervous now, and he'll be looking forward to your advice on how to get out of this jam."

"Good work Bobby. See if you can get me a copy of the report. I will follow up next week. I don't think at this point John will need very much encouragement to sell. And if this acquisition goes as smooth as it appears, I'll sweeten the offer I made to you. This will be a big catch for me."

Chapter 12

As part of Dee Dee's protective umbrella, all of the emails on Whit's company account also came up on her computer. And her early morning ritual was to scan all the incoming emails flagging, deleting, and sometimes even responding to them in his name. In this way she could preempt any problem issues or allow certain communications to appear on his desktop. Because she managed so much of the email traffic, Whit had almost no action to take on anything that came in through the system. In fact, he rarely read his emails. Whenever a request for an appointment came in, Dee Dee would respond in his name and advise the sender to submit a request to his secretary for an appointment. In this way, no one ever got an audience with Cogswell unless she wanted them to meet with him. And it also enabled her to have control over his activities and decisions, without his knowledge or involvement.

Chapter 13

In the basement of a nineteenth century tenement building on Mulberry Street sits the lower Manhattan landmark Grotta Azzurra, a restaurant that Frank Sinatra, always considered his favorite. Sitting at a small table near the open kitchen are Don Davino and Sid Wyse, CEO of Two Wyse Guys.

Wyse had arrived in his stretch limo from his Bronx headquarters to the Little Italy restaurant. His flashy attire was in stark contrast to Don's expensive rack suit of understated elegance.

For the first hour the two men ate crusty Italian bread, dipped in herb-flavored, cold pressed, extra virgin olive oil and sipped red table wine from a pitcher filled with sliced peaches. The conversation consisted of small talk and generalities regarding the retail economy. When they finally got around to look at the menu, Sid commented on the prices and quipped that he was glad that he was the guest and not the host today. This slow dance continued throughout the dinner courses and finally when the espresso was served, Don got down to business.

"Sid, we've been tough competitors for many years, but we have always treated each other with respect. I'm getting tired and I want to get out. Unfortunately, Dominic Jr. doesn't have the fortitude to run the operation, so I'm thinking about selling the company. My goal is to keep all my family employed well into the future, so I have to structure just the right deal."

"Whoa. I wasn't expecting that to come out of your mouth. I was sure you wanted to buy us out. Taking over your company would make us the largest independent discount retailer east of the Mississippi. It would also require us to come up with a shitload of cash. Although I'm getting excited just thinking about it, there are too many insurmountable obstacles.

"For one thing. And I mean no disrespect to you, Don, but there is no way I could have your two sons working in my organization. They don't have your people skills and they would be too disruptive. And I hear that the kid that married your daughter is an overpaid lightweight. What would I do with him? But the real problem is financing a deal this big. Confidentially, we don't have the profitability to warrant that kind of debt. If you want to sell off a few stores at a time, we could consider that. Of course that would take years."

"Sid, I don't have years. I want to come up with a solution that can be completed this year."

"Don, is something wrong? You know, you don't look so good. You have some kind of a serious health problem?"

"No Sid, I'm OK. I'm just burned out. My wife wants me to retire and move to Florida. She doesn't want to live through another winter like this last one. And I'm almost ready to make the move, but I have to be sure my entire family is cared for. With the store managers, shift foremen, warehouse staff and all, I must have fifty nieces, nephews, cousins and second cousins working for the company.

"But tell you what, Sid. Now that I know your interest, your concerns and your limitations, let me think about it and come up with a plan that fits my agenda and will be workable for you. We'll get together for dinner in about two weeks. But next time you pick up the tab, you cheap prick."

Chapter

14

Dee Dee was sitting in Whit's office early on a Friday morning going over the week's activities. He was troubled by a few things and commented to her, "Dee Dee, in my meetings with Shawn, he has been advising me to expect solicitation calls by account reps from advertising agencies looking to pitch our business. And yet, I have not met with one such company. Why is that? Are they not interested in our account?"

"Whitney, I get calls every day, plus material in the mail from these vultures. You're not prepared to evaluate an offer from one of these agencies, nor are you in a position to discuss the terms of any potential deal. As I keep telling you, my job is to protect you from the predators that want to take advantage of you. And it's not just the ad agencies, but other vendors, media reps and our internal staff, as well."

Dee Dee had been dieting lately, so she was looking good and feeling better about herself. And it was showing in the newfound authority with which she spoke. "You have set high goals for yourself. If you want to grow in this job and be successful, you have to concentrate on your responsibilities and listen carefully to your advisors. Shawn and I are the two people you can trust the most."

"Dee Dee, you are taking this far too seriously. No one is going to take advantage of me. I am a college graduate with strong management skills. I want to meet with other ad agencies to determine if we are in fact getting the best possible results from Image Concepts. I am still questioning their strategy. I could learn a lot from these account representatives that are looking for our business. Let me make the decisions about who gets an appointment with me."

Now Dee Dee was getting angry. She stood up, put her hands on his desk and leaned over into his space. "Look, Whitney. Don't delude yourself. You've been sheltered your whole life, and that college degree is worthless in this cutthroat world of business. You need to develop street smarts, which you sorely lack. And just by you making a comment like that tells me you're not ready to take charge."

Whit was taken aback by her aggressive move and scolding. She had never been that close to him physically. Instead of making eye contact, he was staring at her breasts and responded, "Dee Dee you look beautiful when you are angry. And your tits! I want to bury my face in them."

Dee Dee stepped back as she was now furious. "Whitney, don't you ever talk to me like that again. You are married to my cousin and close friend Lucille. I am outraged that you would even think like that." And with that, she stormed out of his office and didn't speak to him the rest of the day.

Chapter

15

That weekend, Cogswell looked up his former classmate Roger Farnsworth, remembering that he was an account executive at a Connecticut advertising agency. He called Roger at home and invited him to meet to discuss advertising.

A very surprised Farnsworth agreed to drive to New Jersey early Monday morning and meet Whit for breakfast. They sat in a booth at The Forum Diner on Route 4, and Whit explained his idea. He wanted Farnsworth to produce and implement a radio campaign offering a trash compactor at a huge discount. He handed Roger the script that he wrote himself.

This is Whitney Cogswell, Marketing Director of Dizzy Don's. Stop what you're doing right now and listen to this once in a lifetime offer. I have a brand name trash compactor on sale at the most unbelievable price of $499! That's almost 50% off the retail price! And for the first 1,000 customers who buy this incredible deal, I'll throw in a year's supply of disposal bags. So get down here right away before they are gone! And don't forget to tell your sales associate that Whitney Cogswell sent you. But get here now and buy this compactor for only $499! You'll never get a chance like this again!

Although the request was unorthodox, the script poorly written, and there was no strategy for the campaign, Farnsworth was not about to turn down the opportunity to break into the Dizzy Don's account. He agreed to produce the commercial, recording Cogswell's voice a few days later at a local studio. He then ordered the media purchase, which Whitney signed off on.

The campaign launched the following Monday. Just before he arrived at the office that morning, Don heard the spot on his car radio. Realizing what was happening he raced into the building and went right to Whit's office. For once Cogswell was in early, preparing a memo to the store managers about the deal. He also wanted to bask in the glory of the soon-to-be successful radio campaign. So he was shocked when Don rushed past Dee Dee, and burst into his office, shouting at him, "Get that fucking commercial off the air immediately. And if you ever do something like that again, I will fire you on the spot!" With that he turned and left Whitney's office.

Whit sat there stunned by Don's anger. Dee Dee hearing the shouting came rushing into his office not knowing anything about the radio ad. When Cogswell explained to her what he had done, she glared at him with a look that could burn through titanium. All she said to him was, "I hope you learned your lesson. From now on you listen to me and don't you do anything you even think I might reject. If you do, *I* will bury you." And she walked out of his office, leaving him to make the phone calls and clean up his mess.

When Shawn heard the radio commercial, he immediately put in a call to Whit. Dee Dee took the call and told him everything was taken care of. She explained that Whit had a very expensive, ill-advised impulse and it was costing him dearly.

Chapter 16

Following his dinner meeting with Sid Wyse, Don did some soul-searching and a lot of deep thinking before he formulated a plan to make his deal work. The next day he placed a call to Todd Christopher, the president of Garfield Community Bank, where his company did its banking. Davino had his account at Garfield Bank when he opened his first store. At this point, Dizzy Don's was the bank's biggest client by a substantial margin.

Christopher was a lifelong friend of John Sassano, a local business owner who founded the bank. Sassano hired Christopher away from Chase in New York, and made him the CEO. Todd was a typical corporate bureaucrat, who always found it easier to say no than risk his status by approving an innovative idea. It was a classic mindset for a small bank president.

Todd Christopher salivated over the prospect of the offer Don put on the table, but it was far too big for his bank to absorb. Garfield could never provide the amount of financing that would be required to transact this deal. He politely declined, but urged Don to find a way to keep his banking business with Garfield.

As soon as Christopher left his office, Don, anticipating Todd's conservative response, put a call into Ben Rusk.

"Hello Don, what a pleasant surprise to hear from you."

"Hi Ben. You have been chasing my account for years. And now I have an opportunity to deliver a lot more than my account, and at the same time have you acquire another bank. Our current banking relationship cannot handle the capital requirements I will need to implement my new strategy. This will create a situation for you to step in. But there are some complications and a few caveats, which I'm sure you will agree to. When can we meet to discuss all the details of my upcoming plans?"

"OK. You got my attention. This sounds important enough, that I'll make arrangements to visit your office tomorrow. Ten AM good? I can't wait to hear what you have to say."

Chapter  17

Two weeks later, the setting was at The Abbey in The Ramsey Country Club. Sid Wyse sat across from Don in one of the stone arched alcoves. He was dying to find out what inventive scheme Don had developed to overcome all of the seemingly insurmountable barriers to doing this deal. He had been tempering his hopes, certain that it was such a long shot, bordering the impossible. But Sid wanted it so bad, he could taste it. And he was hoping Don wouldn't play the same small-talk charade this time around.

But Don surprised Sid and delved right into the terms of his plan. Two Wyse Guys could acquire the Dizzy Don's chain for $150 million. The Davino family would retain all the real estate and lease back the buildings to Wyse. The Wyse brothers would put up a good faith personal deposit of 5% paid over three years. The Davinos would finance the balance of the deal, leveraging the emerging company as collateral. Don would throw off most of the paper to Rusk's bank, through a bond deal his bank would set up. Wyse would provide employment contracts to all the Davino family members, with the exception of Donny, Angelo and Whitney Cogswell. Don Sr. would remain as a consultant for two years to ensure a smooth transition.

Sid couldn't believe that Don had found a way to overcome every one of his caveats. His eyes gave away his excitement, but he immediately tried to reduce the asking price, to which Don replied, "It's not an asking price, it's the selling price. And it's very fragile. Once exposed to the light, it perishes in one hour. Now shake hands with me, because this is the best deal you will ever see in your life. But you're still paying for dinner. And the wine we're drinking is $225 a bottle."

Chapter
18

Dee Dee came into Whit's office and told him that Don was summoning him, along with Donny and Angelo to meet in his office in fifteen minutes.

Surprised by this request for the three of them to meet with Don, Whit asked what was going on.

"Whitney, I'm as surprised as you are, but it must be something big. I asked the other girls and no one has a clue. The only thing I know is that Don has been exchanging lots of phone calls with Sid Wyse. This meeting may have something to do with those phone calls. Assuming that's the case, let me fill you in on Two Wyse Guys."

Dee Dee then proceeded to give Whit a primer on everything she knew about Sid Wyse. He was a bargain-basement retailer, who got joy out of squeezing nickels. He grew up in a poor Jewish neighborhood in the Bronx, and retained the mindset and philosophy taught and practiced by his elders that spending money caused cancer. He would always have a short-term focus, being thankful for even the smallest amount of profit he could turn. Whit just sat there in awe of her knowledge of their main competitor.

When the boys were gathered in his office, Don made the big announcement.

"Well, I just sold the company to Sid Wyse and his brother."

"Dad, are you outta your fuckin' mind? What do you mean you sold the company? What about us? What are we gonna do?"

"Dominic, talk polite. You're supposed to be a businessman. I've provided for everyone, and you are going to have a very big role in my new plan. So you'd better start acting like an executive, or I'll make Angelo president of both of the new companies we're starting."

"Whoa, whoa. I didn't mean no disrespect. I guess you sorta took me by surprise, at's all."

"You're supposed to be my real estate expert, so nothing should ever take you by surprise. And if it does, you never show it.

"Now here's the deal. Two Wyse Guys is taking over all our stores. We keep the real estate and lease the buildings back to them. And we leverage the equity in the land to build a huge real estate dynasty.

"Angelo, you will run a property management company that we set up for the existing buildings and adjacent properties we own, plus everything we acquire in the future. And Donny, you will start building a commercial real estate portfolio with our existing holdings as a base.

Seeing Cogswell totally lost and confused, Don addressed him, "Whitney, I have plans for you as well. I want my daughter to have everything she ever wanted, and there's just no way you're ever going to do it on your own. And you've proved that beyond any doubt." Whitney was offended by the comment but he didn't let it show.

Don continued, "So here's your deal." Although troubled by Don's low opinion of him, and being disappointed about losing any opportunity to take over the running of the appliance chain, Whit was still anxious to hear about what Don had in mind for him.

"The entire plan that I just outlined, the buy-out by Wyse, the leveraging of all the existing property and the acquisition of new real estate deals will all be financed through Garfield Community Bank. Since we're funding Wyse's acquisition, they will be moving their banking to Garfield, as part of the deal. And you will be Garfield's new Vice President."

At that point Donny jumped in, "Wait a minute, How the fuck . . . excuse me. How can Garfield finance all of this? They're way too small."

"Ben Rusk is taking over Garfield Community, so the capitalization will not be a problem. At some point in the near future, Todd will go to work for Ben at Ramapo Interbank. This will create the opening for Whit to become CEO at Garfield and service all our accounts. And maybe, just maybe, when everything is in place and running smooth, I can think about retiring."

"Pop, you really think Whitney here can run a bank? He can't run the marketing department without Shawn holding his hand. Look how he fucked up, eh messed up that radio campaign."

"Don't you worry about Whitney. Todd is going to train him. Dee Dee will go to Garfield with him and she will assist him with the new job. And he will get plenty of support from Rusk. He controls everything at all his banks.

"And Whitney, this is your last chance to make it with our family's help. You pull a stunt at the bank or make a serious blunder, and you'll get fired. Ben Rusk has absolutely zero tolerance for insubordination of any kind, or incompetence for that matter." And with that comment, Don ended the meeting.

Whitney just sat there trying to figure out how he was going to benefit or even survive from this seismic shift in his career. Would there be any way that he could execute his ultimate goal and get back on the track to the president's suite?

Chapter

19

"Dee Dee, what the hell do I know about running a bank? I am just getting comfortable managing the marketing department, but a bank? How can I be responsible for transacting deals in the millions of dollars? This idea that your uncle dreamed up is insane. I hate to admit it, but I will really be in over my head in this job, and I am scared to death of failing. Don said there will be no redemption if that happens. Dee Dee, I am going to need a lot of help to make this work, especially from you."

Dee Dee felt good about Whitney's newfound dependence on her. She was finally confident that he would listen to her every word, and not go off and do something stupid again. "Relax Whitney. Anything is possible. You will be surrounded by smart people, and everything will work out just fine. And I'll be right there to help you. Look how easy it's been with the marketing. You went from zero experience to managing a multi-million dollar budget. You've done it by utilizing Shawn's expertise and my support. It will be no different at the bank. Also, keep in mind that Ben Rusk is going to look over your shoulder and make sure you don't make any disastrous decisions."

"What should I know about Rusk? Is he a fair guy?"

"Ben Rusk is a self-made man. Instead of a wife, he married the bank he established. He is driven, and expects his people to work extremely hard. And if they do, he is very generous with them. If they come up short of his expectations, he can be deadly. But we're going to succeed. I'm excited about the challenge, and so should you be."

"God, I wish I had your level of confidence. And speaking of Shawn, what will happen to him? I had better call him and let him know what's going on."

When Dee Dee went back to her office she thought about how Whitney had finally shown his vulnerability. She was glad that she was put in a position of strength to safeguard him. And she vowed that she would do everything possible to make him successful.

Chapter

20

For Shawn and Laura, Friday evenings were reserved for their Date Night. After a busy week, they enjoyed a quiet dinner with a bottle of fine wine at one of the many local BYOB restaurants that New Jersey's archaic alcohol control laws had created out of necessity. By severely limiting the sale of liquor licenses, the existing ones had an inflated value that often ran into the millions of dollars. So it was more cost effective to run a small restaurant without a liquor license and let patrons bring in their own beverages. It deprived the restaurants of the markup from wine and liquor. But they made up for it by raising their food prices.

On this particular Friday, Laura had taken the afternoon off to play golf with a couple of girlfriends, and she planned to meet Shawn at Radicchio's in Ridgewood for dinner at 7 PM.

Laura arrived first, had the waiter open her bottle of wine and pour her a glass. She was snacking on the bruschetta appetizer when Shawn came in.

"Sorry, I'm late" Shawn said as they exchanged their customary kiss. "It was a killer day, and not a good one. In fact, it's Black Friday."

"Shawn, you look completely stressed. What happened?"

"Well, I'd love to blame it on the traffic from the Bronx, but that was just the final serving of anxiety to end my day from hell."

"What were you doing in the Bronx? You didn't tell me you were going into the city."

"It started with Dee Dee's call for me to meet Whit for lunch at Siciliano's in Glen Rock. It has become his favorite restaurant. He thinks because the food reeks of garlic it's authentic Italian. But then what can you expect from someone named Cogswell IV. Anyway, as soon as I sat down, he started hitting me with one shock wave after another. First, he told me that Dizzy Don's was being sold to Two Wyse Guys."

"Oh my God, no!"

"Wait, there's lots more. Then he explained about the convoluted real estate plans. And finally he told me that he was becoming the VP and eventually CEO at Garfield Community Bank. Can you believe that?

"My response after that devastating news was 'What about Image Concepts? Where do we fit in with all this?' And he suggested that I should accompany him back to the office to meet with Don.

"Don confirmed all this, shedding more light on it, but not much. He then told me that he had arranged for me to meet with Sid Wyse at four today. So I got in the car and drove to the Bronx to meet Sid. Driving over the GW Bridge, I could see the westbound traffic already building up as the tired masses began exiting the city for the weekend. "Sid was his usual obnoxious self. He told me he saw no reason to change agencies, but that Don insisted he meet with me to discuss Image Concepts taking over his advertising account. Sid made sure he reminded me that we turned him down when he wanted to work with our firm. He relished the chance to let me know it was payback time, and there was very little chance that we would get the business now. In deference to Don, he asked me to put together a proposal and come in next week to make the presentation."

"Oh, Shawn, this is our worst nightmare coming true. What are we going to do?"

Chapter 21

Shawn had experienced his share of crises, and he has always survived because he views them more as opportunities than disasters. And he sees failure as a learning experience. So at 8 AM Monday morning, he strolled into the offices of Dizzy Don's. He stopped by Dee Dee's desk and asked her to set up a meeting with Whit as close to nine as possible. He then went down the hall to Donny's office, where he found him sitting with Angelo, chatting over coffee. Angelo greeted him first. "Hey, it's Shawn DiPisa paying us a visit. Tell me Shawn, how does an Italian boy like you get a first name like that?"

"I'm not exactly sure Angelo, because I wasn't there. But my dad told me that he and my Irish mother argued all the way to the hospital over what name they would select if it were a boy. In the delivery room, they settled on Shawn, an Americanization of Sean, which was her choice. The real fun was when my dad called his mother in Italy to announce the birth of her grandson, and the name they selected. My grandmother was shocked, and commented, *"Lo avete nominato Shawn? Ma è così ebraica."* You named him Shawn? But that's so Jewish.

Laughing, Donny replied, "That's a funny story, Shawn. So what brings you around so early in the morning?"

"I've got some questions about your new real estate venture."

"Shoot."

"Frankly, I'm looking for new business opportunities. I know you have some vacant land. Are you planning to develop that land with commercial or office buildings, and if so, will you market them for sale or for lease? Are you planning to acquire additional properties? Will you resell them or lease them? What I'm trying to determine is, will you need the services of a top flight marketing agency?"

"Honestly, Shawn, for right now, all we need is some help with the name and maybe a logo. And we will need business cards and a simple website. We are going to do all the things you're asking about, but it'll take some time. Down the road, we will definitely need your services to help us lease and sell buildings. But for now, we're talking peanuts for fees."

"Hey, I like peanuts. They're better than no nuts at all.

"And Angelo, what about this new property management company? Are you going to just service the Wyse stores, or are you going to be looking for other properties to manage?"

"Just like Don said, we'll start out small and expand as we go. For now, I will also need business cards and stuff, and maybe a website. But Shawn, none of this is going to come close to what you do for our retail business."

"I know that, but I'm thinking survival here. I've got to grab anything that moves. So why don't we schedule a meeting to figure out exactly what you need, and I'll get to work on it. I'll call you in a couple of days and get it set up. In the meantime, be thinking of names you'd like to consider for your two new ventures. And I'll think of some also."

Before going to Whit's office, Shawn stopped in to see Don, Sr. and asked, "Don, what are my chances of getting the Wyse account?"

"I will put some pressure on him to give you the business, but I can't force it. He's a scumbag, and you know it. So even if you get the account, he'll squeeze your balls and make sure you don't make any money from his business. If I were you, I'd go find some other clients. You're smart and very creative. You should have no trouble getting new accounts."

"Don, I wish it were that easy. People are so afraid of change, that even if they're getting lousy work with terrible service, and paying too much, they'll swallow all that rather than go through the pain of moving their account to a new agency. But you can be sure, I'll be going after any client that I think I can land.

"And as an aside, I'm just not understanding why you are so abruptly selling this successful retail operation. Don, what's really going on?"

"Shawn, I think Dizzy Don's has seen its best days. Yes, we are still growing, but the margins get thinner each year. We keep opening new stores, and barely improve our bottom line. And the big box stores are getting so aggressive that they are starting to kill chains like ours. I just decided that the time was right. In another couple of years Sid Wyse will be in no position to buy me out. It's a mistake for him to do it now, but he can't see past his ego. He thinks he won. It's too bad you're going to suffer from this, because you've been a big part of our success. But that's business. I will tell you that I will do everything I can to help you get new customers. I'll try and lean on some people I know, and you can always use me as a reference."

Dee Dee then came and got Shawn and brought him to Whit's office for their meeting.

Shawn got right to the point. "Whit, I'm looking for solutions here, so my company can survive. Unfortunately, the loss of this account will spell disaster."

"Shawn, here is what I know. The transition will take place over three months, and then it will move to Wyse when the name changes. So you've got ninety days to come up with a client or two in order to replace us, unless you get Sid's business.

"I am moving over to Garfield National within the next two weeks, and I am sure I can get you some work from the bank. As far as I can tell at this point, they do not run much advertising."

Shawn left the building and reflected on what he accomplished and where his agency stood. He would gain three small accounts, which combined would not replace one month's income from Dizzy Don's. And as expected, there was almost no chance he would get the Wyse business. Image Concepts was in serious trouble. He had to find a way to survive.

Chapter

22

When Shawn, accompanied by Laura, walked into Two Wyse Guys offices, he looked around at the layers of dust, the piles of papers on all the shabby desks, and the sullen attitude of everyone in the building. As he made these observations, the thought struck him. And made him wonder how anyone could possibly be productive in this environment. He could see Laura wrinkling her nose at the stale odor of the place. And he questioned himself that the presentation he was carrying under his arm was way too slick and professional for a sleazy company like this. His hope, of course, was to wow Sid with a dazzling creative pitch. However, he knew he had no chance to overcome Sid's pre-disposition of rejecting him.

The receptionist, who was wearing a coffee-stained housedress, pointed to Sid's office door and told them to go right in. When they entered the office, Sid was hanging up the phone. He took his cigar out of his mouth, and ignoring Shawn, smiled broadly and said to Laura, "Hiya doll face, I'm Sid." He then invited them to sit across from him at his own desk, which was every bit as dust covered and cluttered as those in the outer office.

Shawn started the presentation by telling Sid that the agency had developed a new brand image for Two Wyse Guys that was similar to

Dizzy Don's successful positioning, but with some important differences.

Before he could go further, Sid blurted out, "What the fuck do I need that for? Just show me the ads" And to Laura, "Sorry, honey."

Shawn was uncomfortable showing the ad concepts that were mounted on 16"x24" gator board across the junk-strewn desk. He was sure he would knock over a Styrofoam cup half filled with week-old coffee or send a pile of papers all over the floor. Sensing his unease, and Sid's flirtations, Laura tactfully took over the pitch and showed the last few boards, which contained the actual ad concepts. Sid, totally ignoring Shawn, said to Laura, "Sweetie, There's some good stuff in there. Give me a week to think about it, and I'll get back to you."

The next morning, Laura came running into Shawn's office to tell him that Sid had just called her and wanted to meet her for dinner that night and discuss moving the account. "He said he has a personality problem with you, and if I handle the account, he would consider giving us the business."

"There's no way in hell that you're going to the Bronx to have dinner with Sid. It's too dangerous. What if you get lost? And besides, I don't trust him. It pissed me off the way he was gushing all over you like a mongrel in heat. He's a sleaze bag."

"Shawn, we need that account like we need oxygen. I can't turn him down. What if I call him and tell him I'm nervous about being in the city at night, and I'll meet him in Fort Lee? And if it means getting the business, I'll be the client service rep, at least for now. We can always hire someone to take over down the road."

At eight o'clock that night, Shawn was surprised to see a set of headlights coming down their long driveway, and then hearing the garage door motor start to wind. He was even more surprised when the back door slammed and Laura came rushing into the den. She was clearly flustered. "That son of a bitch. Before we even ordered, he propositioned me! I can't believe that he could think that I would sleep with anyone, especially a fat, greasy pig like him. I wanted to kick him in the groin, I was so mad. But I got him good. I stood up and shouted loud enough for the whole restaurant to hear, that there was no way I would have sex with him, and he can take his account and shove it up his ass. And I stormed out of the restaurant. It felt really good to see him squirm. But now we're in grave trouble. How are we going to survive? Shawn, I'm really scared."

Chapter

23

The next morning Shawn called Don, and without going into detail, told him that they were turned down on the Wyse account. Don was disappointed but not surprised. He asked Shawn, "You want me to call him and squeeze his balls a little harder?"

"No. It's a dead deal. What you could do for me is call Ben Rusk and recommend me for his advertising business. At this point, he owns a slew of banks."

"Shawn, I will certainly make that call, but understand, Ben's philosophy is to grow through acquisition, not marketing. But I'm sure he could throw you something."

"That would be great Don. If I can get in front of him, I will convince him that he needs a strong multi-media branding campaign."
That afternoon, Don called Shawn and gave him Ben Rusk's private cell phone number. He said, "Try him now. He's expecting your call. But then don't use that number again, unless Ben tells you to."

Shawn immediately dialed Ben's number and explained to him that he wanted to come in and convince him that he should be using branding and marketing as a cost-efficient way to grow his banking operation.

Ben responded "Look Shawn, I don't really need an advertising agency right now. I know you've done a great job with Dizzy Don's. They wouldn't be where they are without your firm's expertise. I'm working on a restructure here that I can't talk about just yet. But there may be an opportunity coming up and I will want to meet with you. Call me in a month at this number and we'll get together."

Although disappointed at not getting an appointment, Shawn was encouraged by Ben's upcoming opportunity. He didn't think Ben would give him any false hopes. But he would have to wait another month to find out what Ben had in mind.

Chapter 24

Dee Dee was sitting on a couch in Todd Christopher's oversize corner office. The décor was typical bank-president traditional, with all the stodgy decorative accessories, designed to make you feel like your money was safe in these grand, hallowed halls. Todd came in and handed her one of the two Starbucks coffee cups he was carrying. "The coffee here is so bad, that I always walk to the corner and get a serious brew."

"Todd, thank you for taking the time to see me. I have a delicate request that I needed to discuss with you personally. As you know, in only three months, we hand our company off to Sid Wyse, and this bank gets taken over by Ben Rusk. Since the plan is for Whitney to replace you as the CEO here when you move to Ramapo, I want to get a head start on the transition. But even before that, as VP he will have to know much more about banking and his responsibilities here."

"OK, so how do you want to do that? I can stay on for a few extra weeks to bring Whit up to speed."

"Speaking confidentially, Whitney is not the quickest learner, and he doesn't have the mindset to absorb critical knowledge. What I'm asking is for you to let me come to work here now and learn your job, and banking in general, so I can better manage Whit when he takes over. This is basically what I did when Don hired him to handle the marketing for the company. I worked behind the scenes with Shawn DiPisa so there were no disasters."

"I think that is an excellent idea. I was also questioning the planned transition period where I indoctrinate him in the banking procedures. But with his total lack of banking knowledge, I'm just not sure it will be enough time. Fortunately, even though we're a small bank, we are very organized in our business structure and processing. And even after I move to Ramapo, I will continue to oversee his activities, so there will be very little chance of a catastrophe."

"Thank you, Todd. You will find that I'm a very quick learner, so I won't be a burden on you. And this plan will save you a lot of grief after the reorg. I'll arrange to start here next Monday. And I'm looking forward to learning everything I can from you."

Chapter

25

About a week later, Ben played golf with State Senator Ed Rothenberg at Hackensack Country Club, where Ben is a member among northern New Jersey's power brokers and business elite. While not an avid golfer, he uses the exclusive facility to entertain important contacts that relish the opportunity to both play and be seen at the prestigious club.

Rothenberg is the Chairman of the NJ Banking Committee and also a ranking member of the Community and Urban Affairs Committee. He had used his brief but successful stint as a federal prosecutor to launch his career in the New Jersey Legislature. He is well respected on both sides of the aisle. And his good looks, political acumen and oratory gifts have him in a strong position for the governorship in the next election. He is also a Hoboken resident, living in one of the converted lofts on Washington Street.

But beneath the veneer of personality and charm, Rothenberg is a hard-nosed warrior, who thinks he's above the law, and his service to his constituents always comes with a price.

After golf, the two men sat on the outdoor veranda adjacent to the putting green and ordered lunch. As they drank beers waiting for their meal, Ben pulled some papers out of his briefcase. The first one he showed Rothenberg was a map of Hoboken. Ben pointed to a block along Hudson Street and said to Ed, "I want you to use Eminent Domain to condemn this block. It's a blight on the city, and I have a plan that will dramatically improve the entire area."

Shocked, Ed replied, "Ben, that's incredibly valuable land. It has a million-dollar view of New York City. I can't move on that property. Whoever owns it will raise holy hell, and the press will persecute us."

"It's owned by the Stankowski family. The old man acquired it years ago for $50,000 after he came over from Poland. He died last year, and his grandkids want a hundred mil for it."

"It doesn't matter if he paid fifty dollars for it. Right now, it's worth their asking price and then some."

"Ed, let me show you what I want to do with the property." Ben then rolled out a set of plans that showed a gleaming, high-rise office tower with underground parking; a retail mall with a rooftop restaurant including an outdoor dining terrace, overlooking the New York skyline; and even a park for the local residents.

Ed was overwhelmed with the plan, but told Ben to negotiate with the family, because there was no way he could pull off an Eminent Domain condemnation. But Ben, expecting that response, pulled his ace and said, "Ed, I've been a major contributor to your campaigns, and you know I'm going to support you big time when you run for governor. So we need to find a way to make this work. So here's some information that I have not shared with anyone.

"Ramapo Interbank is going public, and we're changing the name to StarTrust BanCorp. All of our banks will drop their individual identity and become StarTrust. And the public offering will allow us to grow over time to the size of Chase or Wachovia. Think of what it would mean to have a bank that size, based in your city.

"And here's a little sweetener to make the deal more enticing. I'm going to give your brother a stock option package that will mature over a five-year period after the public offering. At that point his portfolio should be worth several million more than it is today."

"Thank you, Ben. I certainly appreciate all you do for me. It enables me to continue to do the good work for the people of the community. And it makes it possible to provide the best care for my brother. What I would like to do is to be able to cash in a small part of the stock as soon as it's issued. This way I can cover some past election debt."

Of course Ben recognized this false gratitude. For the most part, Ed's brother's care was paid for by the government. And this slush fund, while it contributed to Rothenberg's reelection efforts, went mostly to his gambling and womanizing expenses.

Ben had an arrangement with Rothenberg that went far beyond his donations to Ed's reelection campaigns. Rothenberg's older brother, Billy had been institutionalized ever since childhood in a private facility on Long Island called North Shore Wellness Center. A fall from a tree had left the then nine-year old boy paralyzed to the point of needing constant medical care. Since Ed was the legal guardian for his brother, Ben was able to deposit cash in Billy Rothenberg's account for Ed to access to both pay for some of his brother's care and also for his personal use. Ben also, on occasion purchased stock in Billy's name when he got an insider tip. But nothing ever came close to the potential of this stock option package.

With that Ben stood up and barked to Ed, "Now you get to work and figure out how you're going to make this land deal happen. This time next year, I expect to be looking across the Hudson at those arrogant New York bankers."

Chapter 26

One month later, Shawn found himself sitting across from Ben in his lavish office impressed by the view of the Ramapo Mountains and the Saddle River Valley. As he looked around the office, Shawn realized his entire agency could fit within the walls of this corner office.

He was nervous, of course, and didn't know how to open the meeting. He brought along his portfolio in a large custom briefcase, expecting the opportunity to present his agency's creative credentials as part of his pitch for the bank's marketing account. But Shawn had learned to never show his samples until the prospect asked to see them. The unusually large briefcase always stirred curiosity and that anticipation worked in his favor. He liked to ask his prospects questions before he told them his story. Getting people to discuss their problems and needs upfront always gave Shawn the key clues on what hot buttons to focus on, and what topics to avoid. However, this meeting was different. Ben Rusk was not about to discuss the bank's marketing plans. Up until now, they did very little marketing.

Ben let him squirm a few minutes while he studied some papers on his desk, and finally broke the silence. "Shawn, I'm glad to finally meet you in person. I've heard great things about you, particularly your creative thinking. I'm going to get right to the point. "The sale of Dizzy Don's is going to leave your agency with a big hole to fill. In fact, if you don't replace that account in the next few months, you're going to be faced with shutting down your company."

Shawn was shocked that Ben knew how dire his situation was. But he was right. Shawn was unable to open a single account since the Wyse deal was announced. He thought people were afraid to sign up with him, thinking his agency might fail without the Dizzy Don's account. However, he wasn't about to admit defeat. "Ben, I appreciate your comments, but I am working on some new business leads. And I want to talk to you about doing work for your banks."

"Let me tell you what's going on here, and why I asked you to meet with me. And this is very confidential. We're about to consolidate all our banks under one umbrella and go public. And to do that, I need to add some really smart people to our organization. With all these banks we've been acquiring, I've got a building full of empty suits. There isn't one marketing executive among them, so how am I going to effectively promote our new banking organization? I need a creative-thinking, savvy expert that knows all the aspects of branding and marketing. I don't need a bureaucratic yes-man to hand out money to an advertising agency. In short, I need you, and I'm offering you the position."

Shawn was shocked by this opening salvo from Ben. It was totally unexpected and he was completely unprepared. He was also surprised by Ben's obvious understanding of the marketing process. Trying to recover, he blurted out, "Hold on for a minute. I appreciate the compliment, Ben, but I can't take a job with you. That's not what I came here for. I have a company to run, and 18 people to support. I'm just not prepared to discuss this."

"Of course you are. You're in a tough spot right now and you know it. I'm not only giving you a lifeline, but an unprecedented opportunity. Your agency's line of credit and your office equipment loans are all guaranteed by your house. If your agency goes down, you lose that beautiful home, which I understand is a really special, custom-built

Dutch colonial on five acres. And you're worrying about keeping 18 people employed?" As he said all this, Shawn tried to hide his shock of this unexpected knowledge that Ben had about his business and his personal situation.

"So here's your solution. Go to your landlord and renegotiate your lease for about half the space. Tell him that if he doesn't work with you, you're going out of business. Believe me, he'll play ball. Then figure out who are the key people that you will need to run a much smaller agency. Your wife, Laura can run it with your remaining clients, and we'll give her enough business to make sure it will be profitable. And you start working for me next month as Chief Marketing Officer. Your package will be about double what you're pulling down with your agency."

Shawn was stunned, but his wheels were turning. Ben continued, "I can read the look on your face and what's going through your mind, and I know you've already accepted the offer. I like that. If my other sycophant executives were able to make decisions without the relentless anguish, I wouldn't have to do everything myself."

Reaching out with his hand, Ben smiled and said, "Welcome to the team."

Chapter

27

Whit was at his desk in his new office at Garfield Community with Dee Dee sitting across from him. The intensive education and transition period had been completed and Todd Christopher had left for his new position at Ramapo National.

Whit was now quietly promoted to CEO. He sat there without a clue about what he should be doing, while she did all the talking. "First, we're going to redecorate this drab office and make it more attractive, inviting and comfortable. This way when you have a visitor, they will be very impressed with the office, and they will have more respect for you.

"Over the last few weeks, I have interviewed everyone here at the home office, as well as the staff at the branches. I have prepared a detailed confidential report for you on each employee, and based on that I am going to recommend some changes. And next week, you will hold a meeting with all the executives and branch managers."

"But what am I going to say to them? How will I answer their questions?"

Without showing her exasperation, Dee Dee responded, "You will study all my reports and learn the names, titles and responsibilities of each executive. I will prepare a set of talking points for you to use. And

I will be sitting right next to you in that meeting. If you get stuck with a question, pass it off to me and I'll handle it."

The following day, Dee Dee was back in Whit's office to review her report. "Whit, as you can see, this is bad. Every branch manager is a smiling goof ball who thinks his primary role is to greet the depositors. None of them can make decisions on any level. And the home-office executives are all clueless. They act like they work at a country club. Without the Dizzy Don's business, this place would have collapsed long ago."

"Dee Dee, you said this would be easy. You told me that I could rely on the knowledge of the people around me. Look, I know I have had it easy all my life, so this is definitely going to be the biggest challenge I have ever had to face. I just cannot fail. What are we going to do?"
"Whit, relax. I have it figured out. Fortunately, there are a few staff members who have shown some initiative. First we will start to replace the branch managers with those that show promise. If they work out, we will slowly purge the executive team, replacing them with the best of these new managers. This will all be done in baby steps, so the reorganization will be smooth.

"I will protect you. You will not fail. So calm down and trust me."

Chapter 28

That night Whit got home, went to the credenza and began mixing his nightly cocktails. As he sat with Lucille, he told her about his new position at the bank. Although he tried to act cavalier, she could see just how worried he had become about being CEO of a bank. She commented, "Listen Whitney, the bank exists because of my father's business, and most of the bank's larger transactions are company-related. My father would never have put you there if he thought you were going to fail. And that's why you still have Dee Dee helping you. She and I have been very close since childhood, so there's no way she would allow anything bad to happen to me, or to you. You can relax knowing she will always have your back."

"You are probably right Lucille. She has been terrific at the Dizzy Don's and I am certain she will be every bit as effective at the bank." After dinner, Whit thought about their conversation and began to realize just where this new opportunity could lead. With Dee Dee's organizational and people skills, plus her quick grasp of any business function, he could exploit her talents to take him anywhere he wanted to go. With his sights set so high, he was beginning to see her in a totally new light.

Chapter

29

Flush with cash, Donny hit the ground running in his quest to amass a real estate empire. He was on the phone with Randy Eigen, a commercial agent who had brokered the deals for many of the family's store locations.

"Lookit Randy, here's my strategy. We own a lot of retail sites, but I want to branch out into other commercial properties. I'm thinkin' like office buildings, industrial parks, and stuff. I got a bundle of upfront cash from the sale of the business, and with my numb-nuts brother-in-law at Garfield Community, I've got a big piggy bank to finance any new deals. But I gotta move fast and quiet. If word gets out that I'm buying, prices will go up. Wadda ya think?"

"Donny, we've had a great relationship in the past, and I would welcome the opportunity to be your broker on these new acquisitions. There are some quality properties on the market, but they are priced accordingly. Most of the bargains are distressed properties, that are either empty or in need of major renovations. And some of them are in locations that are no longer desirable. I would recommend that we focus strictly on the blue-chip inventory, and I will negotiate the best deals for you."

"Nah, that's not where I wanna go. Us Davinos have a knack for turning horseshit into whipped cream. You sold us a couple of properties that you thought were dogs, and we ended up very successful with them. You scope out the best of the crap properties and show them to me. I got an eye for this stuff. If I like any, then we'll negotiate the shit out of them. And that's how we'll make some serious coin."

"Donny, that is a very high-risk strategy, and particularly now that you are branching out and diversifying, I would urge you to play it safe with some quality acquisitions. Gain some experience with a few other types of properties. And then you can build a strong, diversified portfolio of commercial real estate. You can always roll the dice as this venture becomes profitable."

"No way. I thought about this, and it's how I wanna go. Do your homework, and let's get it rolling."

Exasperated, Randy recognized the flawed strategy, but also saw the opportunity for huge commissions. He had no choice but to say, "OK. I'll do my research, and have several property descriptions emailed to you later in the week. Next Monday morning, my driver will pick you up and we'll visit the locations you choose from the list. I look forward to seeing you then."

Chapter

30

Dee Dee buzzed Whit. "I have James Killington on the line. He says he knows you and that it's personal. Should I take a message?"

"James? He is a frat brother from college. You may put him through."

"A voice from the past. James, how are you?"

"Whitney, my friend. You are a bank president? I am duly impressed. Back in college, I had been convinced that you were going to become a tennis pro and be kept by some wealthy housewife who was bored, but attractive.

"But let me tell you why I am reaching out to you. I am launching a business right here in New Jersey, and when I came across your name, I just thought that I should give my banking account to one of my fraternity buddies. That is what it is all about, is it not?"

"That sounds great, James. We would love to help you. Tell me about your venture. Better yet, why not discuss it over lunch."

James responded to the invite with a better alternative, "How about if I come by at the end of the day today, and we go out afterward and knock back a few beers."

Later, when James arrived at the bank, he was directed to Dee Dee's desk. Even as he walked up to her, she began to scrutinize him. The shaggy hair, jeans and black tee shirt did not measure up. At least he's wearing a sports jacket, albeit a Walmart special, she thought. Dee Dee showed him into Whit's office, where the two men shook hands and hugged. While they sat and talked, she left and went to a back window to look over the parking lot. As best she could tell the only auto there that was not one of the staff's cars was an old Chevy Vega. It looked like it hadn't been to a car wash in several years, but it apparently had intimate contact with several other vehicles recently.

Later the two men sat at the bar in Taps Saloon and ordered Buds. When asked about the new business venture, James explained that he had an opportunity to acquire a revolutionary green product that improved the performance of toilet bowls while saving enormous amounts of water. "It is not sexy, but the margins are out of the ballpark," explained an excited James. "I have got an investor that will put up a half million dollars for the manufacturing costs once I have the patent rights under my control. I already have thousands of units presold, and a pipeline of customers ready to commit. So I need to open a checking account, sign the lease for the space and buy some supplies. I can run this for a couple of years and cash out with millions." He then showed Whit a sketch of the product, explaining how it worked. "I have been working with the inventor for almost two years now, so I have a lot of sweat equity invested in this project. At this time, the only thing between me and a successful launch is $50,000 to acquire the patent. After that, my only obligation to the inventor is to pay a royalty on each unit sold."

Whit asked, "Would not the investor put up the fifty K? It must be a fraction of what he is prepared to inject into the business."

"If he puts up the front money, then it will be his deal. I would be left out of it completely. If I own the rights, I am protected and that is why I have the contract with the inventor. He would rather get 50 thousand up front and a royalty on each unit sold over the next five years. And of course, the investor does not know how much I am paying up front for the license."

"Ok, James, here is what we will do. Come in tomorrow, and open up your checking account. Then get me a copy of the patent and your agreement with the inventor, and I can arrange a loan with the patent license as collateral."

After a few more beers, Whit excused himself and said he had to get home. He picked up the check, and both men left the bar.

The next day, James was back at the bank with the paperwork, and opened up an account. Whit looked over the documents, and told James he would have the loan note and the check ready for him the following morning.

After he left, Dee Dee came into Whit's office, and shared her apprehension about Killington and his deal. "Whitney, I don't think you should go forward with this loan. I have a bad feeling about this guy, so you need to listen to me."

"Relax, Dee Dee. I appreciate your concern, but James and I are close. Well, we were close in college, and last night we picked right up where we left off after school. He is onto something big, and in a mere couple of weeks we will have over $500,000 in that checking account. After that, as he starts making sales, millions will flow through the account. Bringing in a client of this potential will go a long way to making your Uncle Don appreciate me."

In exasperation Dee Dee responded, "I'm still not convinced. Did you think about what would happen if his deal blows up? So please give it some more thought before you hand him that check tomorrow."

"I have the patent paperwork for collateral to back up the loan. It will be fine."

Chapter

31

A few weeks later, a very angry Dee Dee came storming into Whit's office. She closed the door and stood over him with her hands on his desk. "Tank Magic just closed their checking account."

"So who is Tank Magic, and why does that have you so upset?"

"Tank Magic is the company started by your college drinking buddy, James Killington. The $50,000 was paid to a Stephen Fisher last week, the person that is supposed to be the inventor. His name is on the patent documents in the file. Someone came to the drive-in and closed the account that had only $100 left in it. So the money is gone. I checked the company's address, and the building is unoccupied. I tried to contact Fisher, and he doesn't exist. I then called the law firm that handled the patent, and they don't even do patent work. The paperwork was nothing more than a fabrication."

Whit sat there in shock. Finally, he said, "Do not worry. I will call some of my other contacts from school and track him down. We have a very tight network."

"Good luck with that." Dee Dee left him in his office to stew, knowing that Whit would never find Killington. He was too good a con. She was dreading what she had to do next but there was no choice but to call her cousin Donny and explain what happened.

As expected, Donny was merciless. "What was that starry-eyed asshole thinking when he gave this creep 50K? Is he that fuckin' stupid not to see Con when it's written across someone's forehead?"

"Look Donny. He screwed up, and you can bet he will learn from it, but rather than making it worse, I've got to get that money back. I need your help with this."

"Dee Dee. The money's gone. The prick is gone. I'll ask around, but don't expect no miracles."

Three days later, Donny and Angelo came into Garfield. They went up to Dee Dee's desk and Donny turned and said to his brother, "Give her the envelope." Angelo handed his cousin a thick envelope, as Donny said to Dee Dee, "There's forty-eight large in there. We got to him before he could blow it all. And don't ask. We gotta go." With that both men turned to leave. Dee Dee noticed that Donny had his hand in his jacket pocket, which looked rather awkward. She then realized that he probably hurt it somehow, but could only guess as to whose jaw ran into it.

She went into Whit's office and without sharing the details, told him that she recovered all but $2,000 of the money James borrowed. She then explained that she would get the money back into the bank's treasury, and that he would have make up the difference through his personal funds and his expense account. This way no one would ever know about the illicit loan transaction and the shortage. "You are off the hook, and I will never tell anyone what happened. But the next time you ignore me and get your ass in a ringer, you're on your own. I am absolutely serious."

Whit sat there amazed at what Dee Dee had just accomplished. He said to her, "I am not going to ask how you got the money back, but I want to show my appreciation. Lucille is in Atlantic City with her mom and her aunts, and will not be back until really late tonight. Let me take you out to dinner." And shifting his eyes to her breasts, added, "And maybe we could go back to your place afterwards."

Dee Dee had started to react positively until the last remark and the lecherous look. She then realized that he didn't really want to show his gratitude, but to make a move on her. She firmly responded, "Whitney, I'm sorry but I cannot cross that line with you." And she walked out of his office.

After Whit left the office, Dee Dee sat there and thought about his advance on her. She had been convinced that he really did want to show his appreciation, despite his clumsiness. That, in itself gratified her, but the exchange also made her think about the sexual side of the offer. He was, after all, a good looking guy. But regardless of that, she had to control her personal needs.

Chapter

32

Ben Rusk sat at the head of the table in his boardroom of Ramapo Interbank. Around the table were the CEOs of the banks he had acquired. These included Serena McCormack, Tom Mitchell, Bobby Willis, Todd Christopher and Whitney Cogswell. Also at the table was Hugo Sanchez, John Youngman and Shawn DiPisa.

Ben looked around the room and addressed the group. "You're all wondering why I called you to this meeting, so let's get right to it. I have several announcements to make and they are going to surprise the hell out of you. But let me start with a stern warning that what I'm going to tell you is highly confidential and cannot leave this room." He then explained about merging all the banks into one large regional bank that would be called StarTrust BanCorp. He announced that he would be the chairman of the board of the new entity, and that everyone in the room would become a member of the new Executive Leadership Team. In the near future, each member of the team would have a new title and be assigned a specific set of responsibilities. One person in the group would be named CEO of StarTrust, and a couple more executives would soon be added to the team. Except for Shawn, and possibly Whit, everyone looked around and speculated that he or she should be the likely candidate for CEO. John Youngman, because of his seniority, assumed that it was a foregone conclusion that Ben would choose him.

While each executive sat there envisioning themselves in their perceived new role, Ben dropped the next decision on them. He told them about his plans to build the new headquarters tower in Hoboken. When asked about the timetable, Ben responded, "We have acquired a square block above the Hudson River, and with the city's enthusiastic cooperation, most of the approvals are already in place. I expect that the construction will begin within a month."

Shocked at the timeframe, Youngman asked, "Ben, how many years have you been working on this deal?"

Ben replied with a smirk, "The project was conceived less than three months ago." Then everyone started asking how the seemingly insurmountable problems could have been overcome and progress made so quickly. Ben continued, "When you want to get something done fast, you develop a strategy, go to the right people, and you use all the necessary leverage and resources at your disposal."

But Ben still had one more surprise up his sleeve. He then told them all that the bank was going public and their loyalty and performance would result in them all becoming millionaires.

The shock waves reverberated around the room as everyone tried to absorb the impact of these announcements. They each sat there thankful for the series of events that brought them into this life-changing opportunity.

As the meeting broke up, Ben reminded them about the importance of secrecy until the public announcements were made.

Each executive left the meeting with just one thought – What's my role going to be? Will I be the new CEO? None of them gave a second thought to the fact that they were about to become millionaires through the IPO.

Chapter

33

Two days later, at a few minutes after 7 AM, Dee Dee showed up at Ben's office unannounced. At that early hour, Ramapo's offices were empty except for Rusk. As she came in, Ben looked up surprised. She quickly apologized for coming in without an appointment, but what she had to say was important and time sensitive. Ben pointed to a seat, and she continued, "Mr. Rusk, thank you for giving me the chance to speak to you. I wanted to urge you to consider Whitney Cogswell as the candidate for CEO." Surprised, Ben responded, "He's probably the last one on my list, except perhaps for Shawn, who will become the Chief Marketing Officer."

"Well, let me explain my unusual request. I know you haven't had a chance to get to know Whit, but he's a really likable person with both ambition and a sharp mind. He has a way of diffusing any volatile situation and can persuade people with an adversarial posture to come around to his side. Even as a total outsider, he was able to win over my cousins, who, let's say, have some prejudices against people of his background.

"But, here's what's really important. My cousin Donny Davino has taken over the real estate for the family, which has already been announced in the press. But what you don't know is the plan to build one of the largest privately held real estate trusts in the country. At the same time his brother Angelo is establishing what will become a huge property management and service firm, covering all of the northeast. In addition, there is the financing and cash flow of the merged Two Wyse Guys retail store chain, all of which Whit is managing. As a family, we're committed to sticking together, which means Whit is going to be the banker for this growing empire. That will easily make him the most productive rainmaker in your consolidated bank.

I know you are bottom-line oriented. Now let me phrase this as diplomatically as I can. There is no one in your organization with any kind of star power. So you won't be giving up any advantage by picking Whitney. And besides, he is the only executive with a hard-charging, results oriented assistant - me.

"Oh, and if you're wondering why he didn't come to you himself to plead his case, I thought it would be a good idea for me to share the family plans with you, before you interview him. I know more of the intimate details than he does. Mr. Rusk, you have my word that whomever you make CEO, Whit will support you, and the family business will stay with the bank. But that enormous amount of rapidly escalating income deserves a just reward."

"But how did you even know about my plans, and what do you know about my executive team?"

"Let's just say, that like you, I make it my business to know everything that affects my world. And that is the bonus you get when you bring Whitney in as CEO with me supporting him. You will see that we are a winning combination that will be critical to the bank's success."

Chapter
34

The lunch ritual went back a few years. On the first and third Wednesdays, the Davino women met for lunch at one of the local restaurants in northern New Jersey. Their choice was always one of the many eateries that didn't have a liquor license, so they could bring their own wine, including some that was homemade. The matriarch, Don's wife Maria liked to say, "A meal withouta wine feeds only the body, but nota the soul."

Lucille always brought her favorite wine Montepulciano d'Abruzzo and she would usually drink just one glass. In addition to Maria, the gatherings were attended by a few of the aunts. Occasionally, some of her cousins would join them, if they could take time off from work for the extended lunch. More recently Dee Dee almost never came due to her consuming work schedule.

In the beginning, Lucille was fascinated by the stories the elder women told about their lives in Italy during the Second World War, and the hardships they endured. They shared their dangerous escapades of how they made cigarettes and sold them to the German soldiers stationed in their village. And they discussed the difficulty of dating in a small town as they grew older, with their parents and relatives always in such close proximity.

The lunches became the highlight of Lucille's life, which was growing lonely, due to Whitney's time away from home. He always seemed to be working, or spending time after hours with his friends from college. And when he was home he was unfocused and inattentive. He devoted his evenings to college basketball brackets, Fantasy Football, and other sports betting programs.

Occasionally, instead of lunch, Maria organized a bus trip to Atlantic City with the church group. The cost of the junket included a free roll of quarters for the slot machines and a drink ticket with the buffet lunch. It was so much fun, despite the late hour that they returned, that the women decided to book the trip more frequently.

On the way home from lunch one day, Maria noted that Lucille had been increasing her wine consumption, drinking more than her usual one glass. When she mentioned it, Lucille responded, "You're right Mom. The wine makes me feel good, and at home I am very bored. Lately, I have been finishing the bottle when I get back to the condo."

"Be careful my dear. The lasta thing you wanna do is be a drunk wife for Whitaney. Maka him taka you out to a club or somating."

Chapter

35

"Mr. Rusk, this is Kevin Ribitski, the project manager at the Hoboken construction site. We're running into a problem with the union council coordinator. He's complaining that the job is moving too fast."

Exploding, Ben shouted, "Well, it's none of his fucking business how quickly we get this building completed. Every day costs me money, and I want to be in that space right away. What does he really want?"

"As a union guy, he wants to keep his men employed as long as possible on each site. He also wants to delay the completion date, so we are forced to pay excessive overtime in order to get it done as soon as possible after the scheduled completion date. The only way to avoid that is to offer him consideration of some sort, if you catch my drift."

"Kevin, bring him to my office so we can come to terms. I cannot delay this project."

"All due respect sir, he won't come up to Mahwah. You'll have to come here to Hoboken and speak to him in what he calls a secure environment."

"OK. I'll be at the site tomorrow morning at 7:30.

The next morning Ben showed up in his limo at the construction trailer at exactly 7:30. Ribitski came out to greet him, and together they walked over to a pick-up truck that was covered in dust. The driver rolled down the window, and without bothering to lower the overly loud radio, reached out to shake hands. "Mr. Rusk, I'm Arnie Cunha. Why don't you come around and hop in the passenger seat." Ben got into the cab, which was every bit as dusty as the exterior. His dark blue suit would suffer the consequences.

Ben started the conversation, "So what's the problem here? We need to move this project as fast as we can to get it done on or before schedule."

"Mr. Rusk, I understand fully, but you see, my responsibility is to my men. I've got to be sure they get fair compensation for their work here."

"Arnie, let's cut the bullshit. At the unions' hourly rates, this isn't about your workers. It's about you and it's about your compensation. So what's it going to take to keep peace, get the job done on schedule, and avoid any unexplained delays or vandalism?"

"Sir, you'll see I'm a very reasonable man. I need 50Gs now, and if we meet the completion date, I get another 25. And just so you know, I've got other people that have to get a bite out of this apple."

"No. That's not how we're going to do this. I'll give you $25,000 now, and for every day you come in under the completion date, I add another $2,000. This way, I'm assured that you're going to bring this project in more than a month early."

"Look Benny, you don't dictate the terms. I run the show around here, and I decide when this job gets done."

"No. You look Arnie. You don't know who I am. But I know that you're just an insignificant little asshole trying to shake me down. You have no idea who I know and what I can do. I just gave you the best deal you are going to get. And in one minute, I'm pulling the plug on that offer. And if I do, you will be off this site in an hour. And you won't get a job anywhere in the northeast, not even with the porta-toilet cleaning union. I am dead fucking serious. Now say, 'Thank you Mr.

Rusk.' And then get this project moving at top speed. And don't you ever even think of fucking with me again.

"Someone will stop by tomorrow with your down payment."

Part II

Unbridled Success Abounds

Chapter 36

The grand-opening extravaganza at StarTrust BanCorp's new headquarters turned out to be one of the most lavish in the history of New Jersey. From 12 noon to 5 PM, every commercial bank customer was invited to join the festivities, along with their families. Even the people living in the neighborhood were all invited. The newly built park adjacent to the office building contained a myriad of attractions for kids of all ages, with free food and beverage stations conveniently set up at along perimeter locations in the park area. The lobby and the bank branch were open for tours and there were free gifts for everyone.

At six that evening after the crowds dissipated, the real party began in the tower's penthouse. This floor was comprised of Ben's office suite, which was more lavish than his former Mahwah office, and included a personal exercise room with adjoining bathroom and shower, a private dining room which had its own kitchen, and a conference room. Immediately adjacent, Ben's secretary Elaine had an office of her own. The rest of the floor contained the glass-walled offices of the Executive Leadership Team, the huge boardroom, and the open area for administration support. Marble floors, teak furnishings, ornate ceilings, and an extensive art collection provided the opulence for this enclave of power. Everything was beyond oversize, and with the low-partitioned cubicles of the assistants, the floor gave the impression of being vast beyond its true size. And unlike other office layouts, the perimeter walls were not completely lined with offices. This allowed the floor to ceiling windows to provide breathtaking views of the New York skyline, the lower bay, and the shoreline of the Hudson River.

The invitation list for this coveted, private event included the president of the United States, the NJ congressional delegation, state legislators, the governor and other state officials, Hoboken's mayor, executives from the bank's commercial accounts, Wall Street investment bankers, plus journalists and opinion leaders from all the major media. Of course, POTUS was not in attendance, but his chief of staff came in his place.

Ben held court in his private suite surrounded by champagne, caviar and exotic hors d'oeuvres. He greeted the choreographed list of individuals, starting with the president's chief of staff, and continued through the selected guests who paid homage to this powerful and successful titan.

When Senator Rothenberg walked in, Ben gave him a warm handshake saying, "Ed, I couldn't have done this without you. Getting the non-conforming variances and permits were difficult enough in that timeframe, but I never asked you how you expedited the land deal without the press swarming all over it."

"Ben, it was easier than even I would have thought. As you brilliantly suggested, I called the Stankowski brothers to my Hoboken office and advised them that there was a plan in place to condemn the parcel. Explaining to them that as constituents, I was looking out for their interest, I urged them to quickly take advantage of the sale opportunity from the out of state buyer, or the property would be tied up for years in litigation. What I didn't know, and those dumb Polacks blurted it out right in my office, was that they were desperate for cash. $10 million now was worth more to them than $100 million in five years, and they didn't have the funds to mount a protracted legal battle. So just using the threat made it all work out." Laughing, he continued, "I even got them to make a contribution to my upcoming campaign. As far as the building department and planning and zoning boards, I just called in some favors, and we got it done. Everyone was salivating over the tax money and job creation this project would bring. And of course, there was the prestige of having a major bank headquartered in Hoboken."

"Ed, I don't care how easy you make it sound, you delivered as promised, and I will keep my part of the bargain. A courier will hand deliver a package of paperwork to your home next week. Your brother will receive warrants for a block of stock upon issuance, plus options for future acquisition at a locked-in price. We are filing our public offering within the next few weeks and early projections lead me to believe you will make more than the amount we discussed. A lot more.

"And I'm not forgetting my pledge to help you with the gubernatorial campaign. When you're ready to announce, I will provide both funding and manpower to support you."

Chapter

With everyone preparing to settle in the new building, Ben called in the members of the Executive Leadership Team for an organizational meeting.

"I've been working on a new organizational chart so you will each have a defined role in this new structure. I used your proven skills to ensure your success in the sector you will run. If this reorg does not work out I will either move you around or replace you with other people.

"Shawn DiPisa, as mentioned before will be Chief Marketing Officer. Serena McCormack, as VP Retail Banking, you are taking over the entire branch network. Tom Mitchell, I'm naming you VP Commercial Lending. And John Youngman, I have a special role for you. And that is to manage the Wealth Management and Trust Service. I picked you for that as you have the deepest level of experience in banking. This is a weak area of the bank, and I'm expecting huge growth from this department under your guidance. And if you're successful, you will be properly rewarded."

Youngman was crushed by this development, as he was certain that he would be named CEO. However, he maintained a stoic face.

"Hugo Sanchez, with his bi-lingual ability and experience in Central and South America will be in charge of International Banking. Todd

Christopher will be taking over the Mortgage and Personal Loan Departments. All of these positions are at Vice President level. And for CEO I have selected Whitney Cogswell. He's being rewarded for bringing the tiny Garfield bank from obscurity to the fastest growing bank we owned before the consolidation. Between the retail business and the rapidly growing REIT, Garfield has become a shining star. As you all know, I reward results. So if you want to get ahead in this new organization, you'd better ratchet up your performance. There are plenty of people who want to take over your jobs."

    With that, Ben ended the meeting and dismissed the team. Everyone walked back to their office with disappointment written on their faces. And to a man, with the exception of Shawn and Whit, they all thought they deserved to be the CEO. They also recognized that the only reason he got the coveted position was the business his family delivered to the bank. But as typical, shortsighted bureaucrats, none of them calculated the portion of their salary and their future share value that would be attributable to the vast profit that the Davino-related businesses was bringing to StarTrust. Instead they were only focused on devising ways to bring him down so that they could replace him as CEO.

Chapter 38

StarTrust's new CEO, Whitney Cogswell now occupied the corner office opposite Ben's suite. Whit's office however, was nowhere near as elaborate as Ben's. In fact, by comparison, it's size and appointments were the same as the other ELT members, all of which were only slightly more upscale than Ben's assistant Elaine's office. Dee Dee had a cubicle just like the other administrative support staff.

Dee Dee recognized that Ben, as expected was still running the day-to-day operation and making all the decisions, while Whit was not much more than a figurehead. She decided that she needed to know more about Ben, so she invited Elaine to lunch.

Dee Dee chose the Gaslight and they enjoyed a background-sharing meal together. They bonded over the fact that both women were single, except that Elaine had been divorced. They each had gone to secretarial school with Dee Dee attending Berkeley College and Elaine graduating from HoHoKus. However, Elaine went on to study at Fairleigh Dickinson and got her bachelor's degree.

Elaine asked about Whitney, and Dee Dee explained the marriage to her cousin, and her uncle giving him a job with the family's retail business. She confided that while Whit had big ambitions, he was basically weak and not prone to hard work, commenting, "He's smart enough, but the fact is, he has no balls. He thinks he knows everything because he has a business degree, but he really has no life experience. He therefore doesn't know how to evaluate risk. He was pampered all his life, and he just assumes that everything will work out in his favor." When it was her turn, Elaine shared her opinion of her boss, saying, "Ben can make things happen faster than any man I have ever known. He finds vulnerabilities in his adversaries, and exploits them. And when he dictates terms, he does not back down. Unlike your family, he's not really caring at all. He is totally focused on business and appreciates success. But if you cross him, he is lethal. No one has survived his wrath."

While both women became closer as a result of the lunch, they still did not share any of their intimate secrets. And Dee Dee did not learn much more than she had already surmised about Ben. They did agree to meet for drinks after work the following Friday night.

Chapter

39

With his insatiable appetite for acquisitions, Ben Rusk kept buying up local banks and quickly became one of the largest regional banks in the northeast. Although StarTrust boasted an extensive network of branches, the retail-banking segment barely contributed to the bottom line. Despite the benefit of visibility, overhead and staffing at all the premium locations sapped profits and required high maintenance from the Executive Leadership Team.

On the other hand, the commercial banking side of the house, thanks to the Davinos, was raking in vast sums of money. Davino Real Estate Trust was closing deal after deal. AD Property Management was already employing nearly 500 people. And Two Wyse Guys, with the help of Don Sr. was adding more stores. The family was also using its clout to encourage their subcontractors to bank at StarTrust. The three companies were responsible for nearly 40% of the profit of the commercial banking division. The Davino family however, was not represented on the board of directors.

With Don Davino's consulting contract expiring within a month, Ben decided he needed to protect his golden goose. Restructuring his Board of Directors, he invited Don Davino and Syd Wyse to sit on the board. They were joined by the bank's corporate attorney, Linda

Honeycheck and a few retired corporate executives that included John Sassano, who had founded Garfield Community Bank. Ben, of course remained Chairman.

Chapter 40

At 6 on Friday, Dee Dee and Elaine entered the noisy Black Bear Pub on Washington Street. The release of the stress-induced energy that built up all week from the revelers celebrating the coming weekend was contagious. The women found a small table in the back, ordered two Cosmos and absorbed the activity. It had been a difficult week caused by Ben's blistering pace and demands for both instantaneous responses and perfection. Elaine, in particular was burned out from the activity level. Apparently she emailed the wrong information to an important bank client, and Ben got an irate call.

After their second round of drinks, the women were both feeling a buzz and then the casual conversation got more serious. They shared more about their personal lives and aspirations. As the crowd thinned, they ordered some small-plate appetizers and another round.

Elaine wondered why Dee Dee got to the office at 7 AM every day, even though her workload was so much lighter. She explained that she comes to the office to get her own work completed before the phones start ringing. She then spends the rest of her day managing Whit and sheltering him from the constant wave of people that want to exploit his naiveté.

When asked about her love interests, Dee Dee explained that she was in no hurry to marry, in spite of the family pressure. She really wanted to find someone really special, and she commented, "Maybe I'm too particular and I really do want to be in a relationship, but I have yet to meet someone that I would consider for a life partnership. There are just no real men out there."

"I mostly agree with you, but if you don't put yourself in position to meet people, you're never going to find the right guy. You are a beautiful woman. However, your appearance sends the wrong signal. It tells men that you are not really interested. Forgive me for being frank, but you really need a makeover."

"Elaine, please tell me what you think. I have no close friends that will give me advice."

"OK, then. Change your hairstyle and your makeup, wear more flattering clothes, and get a personal trainer. Everyone has one now. With a good coach, you will get your body looking better and your whole attitude will change."

"I really like what you're saying and I've never thought about changing my looks. It does sound exciting, but I don't want to be constantly hit on by all these guys that think the world revolves around them. They're either macho jerks or helpless wimps, and they don't really know how to treat a woman. Even the guys in the office don't have a clue about how to please us. And none of them respects women."

"Amen to that," Elaine said, tipping her glass to Dee Dee. "Respect is important. I always thought Ben respected me for my loyalty and all the personal time I put in for him. And yet there's never even a glimmer of appreciation. As an example, I am always in the office every morning at eight, and often work till nine or ten at night, and he never even offers to pay for my dinner. He just expects that kind of commitment. And you would be shocked at what he spends on himself. It's often thousands a week. I know because I manage his expenses and pay those bills from a separate checking account. He wants no one in the bank to see those charges. He doesn't even see them himself. And not once in all the time I've worked for him, has he suggested to me to have dinner and put it on his expense account."

"Wait a minute, Elaine. You're an executive secretary. You make decisions in that role, and you shouldn't have to get permission from Ben to pay for your dinner. When I work late hours, I have always charged my dinner to the company. Whit has never told me to do so, because men just don't think of it. They would certainly expect us to get reimbursed, given all the time we put in. Tonight, given the week we've had, you're picking up the tab for our evening out. And when the charge comes in you will approve and pay for it like every other expense."

Elaine faltered, saying, "Oh, I can't do that. I've never done that."

"Bullshit! How many nights have you worked late this week alone? And besides, Ben respects people who make decisions. I'm sure he thinks you are already taking reimbursement for your dinners." That comment pushed Elaine over the top, and she charged the entire bill.

After that, Dee Dee and Elaine started going out to lunch and dinner regularly, but charging the bank for their expenses only if they worked after hours. And Elaine was loving this self-appointed reward system for all her extra effort. During this time Dee Dee was taking Elaine's advice and making small steps at improving her looks. At lunch one day Elaine said, "I have a surprise for you. This Saturday we're doing a spa day and it will be my treat."

When they entered the Fountain Spa, Dee Dee was overwhelmed by the luxury of the facility. They spent the day getting facials, massages, manicures and pedicures, hair styling, and a consult for Dee Dee on weight loss and fitness. Dee Dee especially liked the massage, her first such treatment. She found the experience both sensual and relaxing. It was the first time a woman touched her body like that, and it made her think about how clumsy men were. It was the most luxuriating day she had ever had, and she left the premises feeling wonderful.

Elaine used her credit card to pay for the charges for both of them, and Dee Dee thought the bill must have exceeded $1,000. So she decided to treat Elaine to dinner. Being concerned that the cost might end up going on Ben's charge account, she advised Elaine that it was far too much to charge to the bank. But Elaine justified the expense by saying "You should see what Ben puts on his account. As I said, you would be amazed at what he spends a week."

The two women continued to go out together with Elaine often picking up the charges, albeit much smaller than the spa day. But Dee Dee being concerned about the potentially excessive perks, also paid for some of the lunches and dinners that they shared.

One morning about six weeks later, a copy of Ben's expense report mysteriously appeared on Elaine's desk, with an extensive list of charges highlighted. Elaine became alarmed, but wanted to explain the expenses to Ben, but he was out of the office that morning. At 9 AM, two staffers from HR entered Elaine's office, advised her that she was being terminated, and escorted her with her personal belongings to the parking garage.

When Ben returned to the office, he called Dee Dee in and sat her down. He asked her to take over the role of his executive secretary while she continued to handle Whit's needs. And he went on to explain that Elaine had overstepped her authority and was far excessive in her personal charges to his expense account. "Dee Dee, let this episode remind you that I am aware of everything that happens here, so don't ever try to put something over on me. I know some of the items Elaine put in benefitted you, and in moderation those charges would have been okay. But she got carried away and tried to hide it from me. If you work late or come in on a weekend, I expect you to charge the bank for your meals. Just use your discretion. Am I clear?"

Dee Dee responded, "I understand, and I accept the position. I will not let you down. And I will not take advantage of the charge account." She then left Ben's office and returned to her desk to arrange for the transfer. She would have to talk to Whitney and explain her new, shared duties.

At lunchtime, when the office was quiet, Dee Dee reflected on Elaine's termination. She was troubled over losing her only female friend at the bank, and saddened by Elaine's loss of her job. In a way she blamed herself for encouraging Elaine, but she also warned her about overstepping the prudent limits of the perks. She also thought about the rewards of dedication to one's immediate boss. She was disappointed that Whit really didn't appreciate all she did for him, particularly her role in getting him appointed CEO. It remained to be seen just how Ben would respond to her efforts, but she really didn't expect much in the way of gratitude from him either. This reflection was hardening her resolve and making her more determined to look out for herself, despite her dedication to Whit.

Chapter 41

Before Shawn moved to his new job at the bank, he and Laura reviewed their client list and decided to drop a few high maintenance clients that generated little or no profit. He then went out and met with all the remaining clients, explained the reorganization, and pleaded with them to give Laura the chance to continue to deliver the agency's services to the level of their expectations. While every client said they would continue, Shawn felt that at least two of them would probably change agencies.

Shawn met with their landlord to renegotiate the lease, and while they were sympathetic to the agency's account loss, they were not anxious to give up much revenue. They knew that Shawn couldn't be too demanding due to his personal guarantee for the life of the lease. In the end, he settled for a smaller parcel with 40% less space, but at a higher rent rate, and a longer lease. The landlord wound up with close to the same amount of money over a longer period of time for the smaller parcel, but Image Concepts had a lower monthly rent to pay. And that was the goal.

Laura promoted two staff members to fill her position of production manager, and Shawn's role as creative director. She then had to lay off more than half the staff.

Both of the Davino's new companies did come through with their projects as expected, but that didn't begin to fill the giant hole that was left by the departure of the Dizzy Don's account. Laura began to make regular sales calls on prospective companies, to try and grow the business. She got lots of promises from prospects that viewed her portfolio favorably, but very little business came in immediately. So even without drawing a salary, the company was burning through its cash and into its line of credit.

Shawn kept telling her not to worry, that new business would begin to come in, and he would soon be in a position to start feeding her business from the bank. Before long however, she had to lay off even more of the remaining staff. When she tapped out the credit line, she had to take money from their retirement fund to pay the company's bills.

All of this was frustrating Shawn, as he felt helpless that he could not contribute to the success of the agency he founded. He was also bored at work because there was not much for him to do. He went to Ben and pointed out that the retail branches were not doing well, in comparison to the commercial business. He recommended that they launch a marketing campaign to begin to build the brand and promote the branches.

Ben brushed him off, saying that he was too busy with a couple of complex acquisitions and wasn't ready to think about marketing.

Chapter

Senator Ed Rothenberg, while watching Monday Night Football in his lush Hoboken townhouse, got a heads-up phone call from a Trenton Times reporter. She advised him that she was writing an investigative report about his relationship with one of his attractive female staffers, who was living part-time in his Trenton apartment. When asked to comment on the story he declined by shouting through the phone, "You are one stupid bitch whose journalism career is about to self-destruct. Do you have any idea of the power I wield? I'll see that you won't get a job writing obituaries for a church bulletin."

Hearing the shouting, his wife Cynthia came rushing into his den to see what was wrong. Gulping the remainder of his cocktail, he grumbled that the Democrats had planted a fictitious story about him carrying on with some bimbo in Trenton. He further explained that as one of the few Republicans in the overwhelmingly Democratic state, he was a constant target of the opposition.

Of course Cynthia knew better. As a beautiful former model working with the State's tourism office, she had met Rothenberg four years earlier at a conference in Atlantic City. At the time he had been married to his high school sweetheart, but that didn't stop him from putting a full-court press on her. She was taken by his charm, his position, and the power he held. Their steamy weekend in the bars, casinos and the bedroom clinched the relationship. Ed quickly divorced his wife and within three months was married to Cynthia.

It didn't take long for her to realize the truth of the axiom, "You live by the sword. You die by the sword." While she used her beauty, her shapely figure and her lively personality to attract Ed to marry her, it wasn't enough to keep him faithful. Once the glow of the conquest had passed, she knew that he needed the constant ego boost and thrill of seducing women. After all, in his position, it came with the territory. He was certain that every woman wanted him, and his narcissism convinced him that he was entitled.

But now Ed faced a potentially catastrophic problem with public exposure of his lifestyle. The story in the Trenton Times was just the tip of the iceberg. And it could severely impact his plans to run for governor.

Chapter

43

On Tuesday morning at 7 AM, Shawn sat in his office reading the anemic reports of the bank's retail business. He was very frustrated with Ben's inaction with this market segment. There was so much that could be done to increase traffic at the branches and generate profits. He had even put together a plan for a full public relations and a local advertising campaign to grow this business, but he hadn't been able to present it to Ben. And to make matters worse, Laura needed some new work to keep her struggling agency afloat. This was a win-win situation and Shawn could not get through to Ben with his ideas.

As Dee Dee walked by Shawn's office, she noticed his depressed look as he scanned the documents on his desk. She walked in and said, "Shawn, you are not your usual upbeat self. I could always count on you to lift everyone's spirits when you came into the office. But lately, you seem distracted. And this morning you actually look depressed. What's wrong?"

"Dee Dee, I'm bored, frustrated and angry. None of what Ben promised is panning out. I'm beginning to feel like a bureaucrat. I'm going stir-crazy sitting in this office pretending I'm busy. And yet there is so much I can do for this company. And Laura is going broke from lack of clients, even after Ben promised her this account."

"Shawn, you have to understand that Ben is very distracted with some of the major deals he's working on, any one of which could be larger than the entire profit of our bank branch network. But let me see if I can help you get the ball rolling."

Within fifteen minutes, Dee Dee poked her head back in Shawn's office, winked and said, "Start implementing the plan for the retail branch promotion." Before he could respond, she turned and went back to her desk.

Shawn immediately called Laura at home and told her to come to his office before she went to the agency.

Chapter

44

After getting his phone call, Laura drove directly to Shawn's office full of anticipation. He walked her through the plan to promote the branch offices, giving her some creative direction for the message, and the look and feel of the advertising. His plan called for newspaper print, and local radio spots in every city the bank had a branch. The plan only contained a rough budget for media, so he asked Laura to research the costs and submit a complete media schedule.

In addition to the advertising, Shawn wanted to run a public relations blitz. Laura suggested that she bring in one of their freelance PR specialists to organize that effort. She also thought the campaign should include some social media. "Let's do a promotion on Facebook and we can generate some buzz with that." Shawn liked the idea and said he would come up with an offer to feature in the promotion.

Laura left the bank and headed to her office feeling giddy. This was a huge campaign, that would easily run over a million dollars, and she was excited. Maybe her little agency would now have a chance to survive. As she drove to her office, she was already planning the first steps.

Shawn felt excited as well. He finally had something productive to work on, and he was going to make this program a huge success. He also had to thank Dee Dee for accomplishing in five minutes what he couldn't do in three months.

He walked down to her office and asked her how she pulled it off. "Dee Dee, how did you get Ben to sign off on this project?"

"It was easy," she replied. "I told him that he couldn't do everything himself, and that's why he had me there. I then explained that with his approval, I could get the bank branch campaign launched while he handled the major deals. And he told me to go ahead and have you implement it."

Chapter

45

It started with a brief story in the Trenton Times on a slow-news Wednesday morning, and by the time the six o'clock news began, it was a full-blown scandal that rocked the entire New York area.

As soon as the story broke, the Associated Press picked it up and put it on the AP newswire. The NY Post, a tabloid that thrives on this kind of titillating news immediately put a team of its own investigative journalists on the case. They also headlined the story on their website.

In Huntington, Long Island Susan Grabenstetter was sitting at her kitchen counter sipping coffee and booting up her computer. Her home page, NYPost.com came up headlining the story about Rothenberg's live-in at his Trenton apartment. Grabenstetter, a nurse at North Shore Wellness Center dropped her coffee cup and screamed, "That fucking bastard!" so loud that it woke up her toddler son, Eddie. After she calmed down, and got her son into his highchair with some Cheerios on his tray, she sent an email to one of the reporters at the Post.

At the same time, Cynthia Rothenberg was getting dressed in her Hoboken townhouse. Ed had left their home unusually early that morning for destinations unknown. The previous evening, after his lame excuse about the inaccuracy and mistaken identity in the news report, they had not exchanged another word, and he later fell asleep on the couch.

Expecting that this day would come, she had already engaged a high profile divorce attorney in Newark. She took out several large folders of documents from her file cabinet, filled a briefcase with them, and left for her meeting.

Being the media capital of the world, New York City loves a salacious scandal, and on this Wednesday evening the city was getting a real blockbuster. All the broadcast channels led with the story of Senator Ed Rothenberg, the powerful Chairman of the NJ Senate Banking Committee, having an extramarital affair with a staffer in Trenton. And at the same time, supporting a nurse and his love child living in Huntington. The story just kept getting juicier. On Fox News, the lead anchor had an exclusive interview with a reporter from the Post. His investigation had already uncovered other women who were stepping forward to say that they had had illicit relations with Rothenberg.
As sometimes happens, the aftershocks cause more damage than the original quake. And this was one of those times.

Chapter  46

On Thursday morning, Fox again led with the latest chapter in the story, which was quickly picked up by the other media. They announced that Cynthia Rothenberg was filing for divorce and would hold a press conference at 11 AM at the office of her attorney.

Nathan A. Moxley had the penthouse office suite at Gateway Center in the revitalized downtown section of Newark. Because he handled so many divorces for sports and entertainment celebrities, as well as corporate titans and elected officials, his imposing offices were designed to accommodate large press conferences.

After the media teams had set up their equipment, Cynthia Rothenberg entered the large conference room through a side office, flanked by Moxley and another gentleman. She was dressed in an understated gray business suit with an ivory silk blouse, and a simple pearl necklace being the only jewelry she wore.

Next to her stood a man that none of the press recognized. He wore an ill-fitting brown suit with the requisite white shirt and a brown and black tie.

By contrast, Nathan Moxley wore a tailored blue suit that was a few shades too bright for the taste of most professionals. It was offset by a light blue dress shirt with a white collar and cuffs, and an outrageous purple and lavender tie with matching braces. His diamond cuff links and tie tack glittered in the camera lighting. He was clearly the star of this performance, and he relished the opportunity. He looked out at the assembled reporters, photographers, cameramen and sound technicians, and beamed. The national prime time news exposure from the next half hour would be the equivalent of a million-dollar ad campaign for his thriving law practice.

Moxley introduced himself, not for those in the room, but for the massive television audience that would see him on the six o'clock news in every living room in the country. He announced that he represented Cynthia Rothenberg, who was filing for divorce against Senator Ed Rothenberg. He went on to explain that the senator's infidelity had caused extreme pain and suffering, shattering her life and destroying the home she provided as a faithful wife. And as a result of the humiliation heaped upon her by an uncaring husband, she was demanding 100% of the assets accumulated during their six-year marriage. This included the large townhouse in Hoboken, the oceanfront vacation home in Deal, the yacht he kept at the marina on Shark River, and his extensive stock portfolio.

After Moxley delivered his prepared remarks with the performance of a seasoned actor, the journalists began directing questions to Cynthia Rothenberg. Clearly nervous, she stepped up to the podium and stated. "I'm too distraught to answer questions today, my attorney will respond to any of your inquiries. I came here today to deliver this package of documents to Mr. James Pippinger, who is a federal prosecutor with the Attorney General's office." With that, she turned and handed over a briefcase to Pippinger, and then left the conference room through the same door she had entered.

This beautifully choreographed move elicited the exact response Moxley expected. The room exploded with a cacophony by the media reps, all trying to get answers to what the portfolio contained. He smiled, stepping back up to the mic as the crowd hushed and teased, "Ladies and Gentlemen, I can't tell you exactly what's in the briefcase, but I do know that Mrs. Rothenberg kept copious records of all the couple's financial transactions, making copies of all records, contracts, agreements, and monetary exchanges carried out by her husband. These included all of the records involving the care and housing of his disabled brother in Long Island."

Knowing that these comments would only serve to drive the news media into a frenzy, Moxley raised his hands, as the assemblage went wild with questions. "I can't tell you any more than that. You will have to direct your questions to the Attorney General's office, once they have had a chance to scrutinize the contents of the briefcase. This conference is over."

Chapter

47

At 10 minutes after noon, Ben Rusk got a call on his cell phone. Very few people had this number, and they only used it in emergencies. The caller advised Ben that Cynthia Rothenberg had just handed over a briefcase to a federal prosecutor at a news conference, and it was being reported on the 12 o'clock news. He had already heard the reports about Rothenberg's exposure for his infidelity, so he was not surprised by the contents of this call.

Ben immediately collected his briefcase and laptop, prepared to leave his office, and without explanation told Dee Dee to cancel all of his appointments for the rest of the week. As he left the garage in his limo, he called his attorney at his private cell phone number, which had similar restrictions to Ben's phone. He told the lawyer he was on his way there, to drop everything and expect him in an hour for a crucial meeting.

Woodrow Horvath was the lead partner of one of Wall Street's most powerful law firms. And dropping everything was no small feat for someone who personally oversaw the legal accounts of some of the largest corporations in the country.

Horvath's office at 125 Broad Street in lower Manhattan boasted views of the entire New York harbor as well as the East River. He was very concerned at the urgency in Ben's voice, and knew Ben would never make a demand like this unless it was extremely critical.

When Ben was shown into his office, Horvath could see the stress in his client's face, which confirmed his suspicion. He immediately asked, "Ben, what's this all about?"

Sinking into a chair in front of Horvath's massive desk, he responded, "Haven't you heard about the Rothenberg scandal? It's all over the news."

"That's what you're upset about? Big fucking deal. Another hotshot politician got caught with his dipper in too many tanks. I know you've been supporting his campaigns, but it's nothing more than a messy divorce. It can't touch you."

"Listen Woody. His wife turned over a briefcase to the federal prosecutor. I can assure you that it contains files with some extremely sensitive and incriminating documents that could ruin me. Actually, they will ruin me. I had a very special relationship with Ed Rothenberg. I facilitated his money laundering schemes, set up his private banking and investment accounts, and lots more. You see, his brother has been in an institution most of his life, and Ed has paid the cost of that care for years. I created accounts and funneled in money to help pay his brother's care and provide a slush fund for Ed's gambling and his other entertainment activities. And I also set up an investment account in his brother's name, and had stock including initial shares of StarTrust, bonds and other instruments deposited into the account, as payback for Ed's ongoing assistance with the bank's legislative needs. Do you have any idea how much I put into that account just to get our building in Hoboken approved?

"And his wife somehow got access to all that information, and with it she will not only take Rothenberg down, but she will destroy me along with him."

"Jeez, Ben, this *is* serious. We need to find out what's in that case, and how bad a hit you're going to take. I think you need to take a brief vacation until the smoke clears.

"Here's what I want you to do. Send your limo back to Hoboken.

Take a cab uptown and do some shopping. Buy a duffel and some beach attire, and ditch the suit. Pay for everything with cash. When you're done, take another cab to the 79th Street Boat Basin. I'll call City Island and have my yacht pick you up at 4 PM, and take you to my cay in the Bahamas. You can chill there until we figure out what they have on you and what we have to do. Before you leave here, call your office and tell them you just came from your doctor and he ordered some immediate rest, or you'll be facing a heart attack. Tell them he is checking you into a private spa for about a week.

"Now get the fuck out of here and let me do some work."

Chapter  48

At about the time Ben was leaving Horvath's office, FBI teams descended on Rothenberg's office in Trenton, his townhouse in Hoboken and the vacation home in Deal Township. Armed with subpoenas, they confiscated all the files, phones and computers at all three locations. Simultaneously, another team arrived at Rusk's office to collect all his files and his desktop computer. Dee Dee tried to stop them, but was told to stand aside or she'd be arrested. This same team then went to his St. Moritz luxury condo in Edgewater and had the concierge open the unit. They then combed the apartment and collected every file they could uncover. They found no computers although his desk had a docking station, but no laptop.

That evening more bombshells started to detonate. James Pippinger, the federal prosecutor appeared on both the local and national news broadcasts announcing the warrants for the arrest of Senator Ed Rothenberg and StarTrust BanCorp Chairman Ben Rusk. Citing a treasure trove of documents provided by Rothenberg's estranged wife, he was moving for a quick arraignment of both individuals, plus anyone else who may be involved in the extortion scheme. He intimated that other businessmen and contacts of the senator would be indicted upon the completion of his investigation.

The following morning, Rothenberg, and his attorney arrived at the prosecutor's office looking to cut a deal. He wanted to quickly put the entire episode behind him before it got any worse. He was willing to throw Ben Rusk under the bus, give up his senate seat, pay a fine and get off with either a suspended sentence or a short stay at one of the country club prison facilities for non-violent criminals.

Pippinger was having none of it. While he had a meek demeanor, he was anything but. He laughed at Rothenberg's gesture and said, "I haven't even begun to investigate this case, but I already have enough evidence to put you away for some serious time. And who knows how many other constituents you've been shaking down. I'll see you at the arraignment hearing."

After Rothenberg and his lawyer left, Pippinger put in a call to Rusk. Dee Dee took the call and explained to him that Ben had checked into an undisclosed health facility on his doctor's orders, after suffering chest pains. When Dee Dee was unable to give him the name of the clinic, Pippinger ordered her to track down his doctor, get the name of the clinic, find Rusk and have him call back immediately. He further punctuated his demand with the comment, "If he doesn't call me, I'll consider him a fugitive, subject to immediate arrest."

Dee Dee immediately called Woodrow Horvath and told him about Pippinger's call and the FBI raid. As soon as he hung up, Horvath called the prosecutor and arranged to meet him later that day.

Dee Dee then phoned her uncle Don and told him what had happened. He said he would come to the bank within an hour and for her to call together the Executive Leadership Team when he arrived. She then went into Whitney's office, where he was meeting with Shawn. Hearing about the Pippinger call and threat, coming on top of the FBI raid, Whit was beside himself. He didn't know what to do. Shawn said, "Look. Ben must be in serious trouble and that could bring down the bank. We've got to have a plan to prevent that." Dee Dee told them that Don was coming to the office to meet with the Executive Leadership Team for that very purpose.

Chapter

49

With everyone gathered in the executive conference room, Don addressed the group. He said, "We're facing a major catastrophe. At this time, we don't know the extent of the action against Ben, but it can bring down the bank. Since he is the face of StarTrust, we have got to put together a plan to protect our brand image."

Tom Mitchell interrupted him saying, "At this point we know nothing. Whatever it is, it's Ben's problem, so we should do nothing."

John Youngman jumped on that bandwagon adding, "I agree. We need to hide in the tall grass until this thing blows over. And we must cancel that ill-advised ad campaign we were about to launch. We don't want to bring any unnecessary attention to ourselves." And just about everyone else in the room nodded agreement.

With that, Shawn jumped out of his seat, stood up and said, "What the hell is the matter with you people? Doesn't anyone have any understanding of communications? While I agree that we need to distance ourselves from Ben's problem, that's not going to happen by us camping out under our desks. We've got to get out in front of this mess and tell the bank's story. We've got a good bank here, and we employ thousands of people, and they contribute to the welfare of every single community we're in. We've got to come out with a blockbuster PR campaign to tell our story. And there's no way in hell, we're canceling the ad campaign. It will be critically important to get people into our branches so we can tell them one-on-one what a great bank we are. We are the Executive Leadership Team, so how about we show some leadership instead of acting like a herd of wimps!"

The room went completely quiet. Everyone looking for someone else to take the next step. Finally, Don broke the silence. "Shawn, thank you for speaking up. I'm glad someone has some backbone around here. What you're proposing is about what I had in mind. There is no way that we are going to sit on our asses while the press tears us apart. Start putting together a communications plan. And for everyone else in this room, start thinking of ideas to contribute to that plan."

Youngman then pounded his fist on the desk and addressed Don. Who the hell are you to give orders to us. I'm the senior executive and the most experienced banker in the group. And I say you're wrong." Before Whit could respond, Dee Dee spoke. "John, be quiet. You're making a fool of yourself. Whit is the CEO, and Don is a key board member. If Whit agrees with Don, then we move forward."

Whit, taking his cue from her, then said, "Thank you Dee Dee. And Don is right. Shawn's idea is the way we're going forward. I want to be proactive, and not be at the mercy of the press. We'll be a better bank when this is over."

When Shawn came out of the meeting, he called Laura immediately and told her to track down Gerard Thompson from Broadside Public Relations and set up a meeting at his office as quickly as possible. He explained the situation and told her the bank needed a full-service PR firm, and not a freelance practitioner. This would be a highly strategic, multimedia campaign that would penetrate the entire northeast. He also told her to have Thompson engage a strong lobbyist he could trust, who had banking experience, to participate in the assignment. When Laura questioned the need for a lobbyist, Shawn explained that he was concerned about repercussions from the state legislature's banking committee. A lobbyist could make some quiet inquiries among their contacts at the state level and also the banking regulators. If there was any possibility of one of these agencies moving against the bank, then they had to be prepared to contest it.

Chapter 50

By the time Shawn hung up from Laura, he was the only one left in the executive offices besides Dee Dee. He knew she was very upset so he went down to talk to her. When he walked in, he could see that she was visibly upset. She asked him, "Shawn, do you think Ben's troubles will bring the bank down?"

"No. We're already too big for that. Of course, we don't know if Ben did anything illegal with the bank's funds, although I doubt it. That could hurt us if it were true. But Dee Dee, we now have very serious problems and I don't want to minimize them. You are going to be under even more stress over the next few months, so I want to help you. The news reporters are going to be relentless. You're going to be getting calls constantly from them wanting to speak to Whitney. They all want a statement from him, since he's the CEO. No one gets to speak to Whit. No one. And I will tell him myself in the morning. Tomorrow, I will give you the name and contact of a public relations executive who will be the official spokesperson for the bank. He will be the only one who speaks on behalf of StarTrust. I will also have you get out a firm memo to that effect to all the ELT members. I will talk to Youngman myself, as he is the most likely executive to ignore the directive. We can't have a loose cannon making a grandstand attempt to tell a different version of our story.

"And if you get overwhelmed, and you most certainly will, please call me. I will help you. We need you to be at your strongest right now, because Whitney will crumble under the pressure. So keep him under wraps."

"I understand how serious this is. And thank you for recognizing my needs right now. I will come to you if I get in trouble. I promise."

Chapter

51

"Ben, it's Woody. This is bad, seriously bad. That angry bitch Rothenberg has built a file on her husband that you wouldn't believe. She has notes on his every move for the past three years. Phone records, hotel bills, plus all of the statements from Billy Rothenberg's accounts. She has even documented how much toilet paper he uses when he shits. And you are up to your ass in it, because so much of it has your fingerprints on it. Most of the money in the accounts traces back to you. She must have hired a snoop, and a good one."

Ben was still in the Bahamas, at Horvath's Key West style mansion on his private cay. What Woody was telling him confirmed his worst fears.

"Woody, how can we make this go away? Who do we have to take care of? If she has as much as you say, I'll be facing years on the farm, and my banking empire will collapse. My entire life's work flushed down the drain because of one vindictive bitch.

"How much does she want? I'll pay whatever it takes to get her to recant her story, and say the files are bogus."

"Ben, this is not about money, not yet. You just don't understand women. Right now she wants to crush Rothenberg's *cojones* into a hamburger patty and fry it. She then wants to humiliate the crap out of him, and put him in jail. After that, she'll be thinking about the money.

This cat is out of the bag, and Pippinger is a no-nonsense investigator. He is not letting go. He's an obscure prosecutor that's been passed over his entire career. And now he has the case of a lifetime with national news coverage, and the chance to bring down two highly visible public figures. You can bet he's planning on trading in his cubicle in Newark for a corner office at Justice in Washington.

"Ben, there's no way out. Come home and face the music, and let's see if we can cut a deal with Pippinger, pay a fat fine and get a minimum sentence. I will try to make any deal contingent on you not getting banned from banking."

Chapter 52

Just before noon, Bobby Willis stopped by Tom Mitchell's office and said, "Let's go to lunch. After that meeting, we've got a lot to talk about."

Tom responded, "Good idea. Let's grab Serena and have her join us."

As soon as they placed their food order, Willis broached the issue. "We have to assume that Ben is toast. He may possibly find a way to wiggle out of this catastrophe, but I think Cynthia Rothenberg has buried him, along with her slimy husband, the Good Senator. That means we're stuck with Whit the Twit. He can't run a bank. He has absolutely no experience."

Mitchell replied, "You're right, Bobby. And you saw John in the meeting, already trying to make his move. He still thinks it's the eighties, but he doesn't have a clue how banking has changed. We have to meet with Whit, and convince him to step down and let us reorganize the bank."

Now it was McCormack's turn to add her two cents. "Before we talk to Whit, we have to get past The Iron Maiden. Dee Dee doesn't let anyone have an appointment unless she approves. And Whit listens to no one but her. He hangs on her every word. Even if we get an audience with him, he will get her opinion before he does anything. Prior to us making any kind of move, let me take her out to lunch and talk to her."

Willis then asked, "You're right Serena, but how does that plump bitch get so much power?" And Mitchell, winking at Bobby, added, "Yea, she is plump, but she does have great tits." With a smirk, Bobby responded, "Oh she's got big melons, but I'll bet her underwear is the size of a parachute."

With that, Serena exploded. "What the fuck is it with you men! You can't see past a woman's breasts. I can assure you that her chest has nothing to do with her power. She is cunning, smart and very ambitious, but you two jerks only see big boobs."

While this trio of executives was having lunch, Don Davino phoned the Board Secretary and told her to call an emergency meeting of the bank's Board for the following evening. He also advised her to cater in food, as it would be a long night.

Chapter

53

J ohn Youngman sat in his office fuming after the ELT meeting. Davino took over the meeting, usurping his position of the experienced senior banking executive. DiPisa, who doesn't know shit about banking, gets to call the strategy. And Cogswell, who doesn't know shit about anything, gets to make the decisions because he's the CEO. Then there's Little Miss Dee Dee, who controls Cogswell, and is really the person with the power. So she would have to become his target. As he began to understand this dynamic, he realized what he had to do to end up on top. Unless Ben was a magician, he was not coming back anytime in the foreseeable future, so the bank really needed someone with his knowledge.

Youngman hung around in his office after hours, knowing that Dee Dee would be the only one left in the executive suite. He walked into her office, sat down and said, "Dee Dee, I can see that you recognize how perilous the bank's situation is right now. And you also realize that Whit is way over his head, and he needs my advice and my knowledge. We both want him to succeed, and I'm here to help. Why don't you wrap up what you're doing and let's go across the street for a drink? We can talk more there."

They walked to Nine, a posh nightspot, and sat in a corner of the sleek lounge. Dee Dee ordered a Pinot Grigio and John had a dirty martini. After he clinked her glass and took a sip, he began to tell her about his years in banking and some of the perceived crises that he overcame with his brilliant strategies. By the second drink, he was on a roll, and Dee Dee hung on his every word. "John, I had no idea you had to deal with so many major issues during your career. I am impressed."

After some additional small talk, and more war stories from John, he said, "Dee Dee, I'm really enjoying this conversation. Why don't I work on some strategic ideas and we can get together again to discuss them? And then we'll bring a plan to Whit. Let's do it over dinner sometime within the next week."

As Dee Dee drove home, she reflected on her evening with John Youngman. He was a distinguished, good-looking guy with gray-blue eyes and a full head of salt and pepper hair. His body was that of a middle age male, although there were some signs that he did use the bank's fitness facility to keep toned.

Unfortunately, his thinking was so old school, nothing like Ben's or Shawn's. Even her uncle Don, who was much older than John, was a more agile businessman. And the entire time, all he did was boast about himself. He never once asked about her. A typical, self-centered, egotistical male. "It was too bad," she thought. He certainly was attractive.

Chapter

54

The following night, with all of the directors gathered in the boardroom, Don stood up to address them. "Ladies and gentlemen, thank you for changing your plans for this evening and attending this important meeting. StarTrust Bankcorp is facing an unexpected crisis of truly monumental proportions. Ben Rusk has been indicted for a myriad of serious crimes, and because he is the face of StarTrust, these transgressions could have a terrible impact on the bank. This board must take immediate steps to distance itself from his actions, and we must safeguard our investment.

"As our first order of business, we have no choice but to remove Ben from the board, and elect a new interim chairman. If there is any remote chance that Ben is exonerated of these charges, we will welcome him back to resume his position. Does everyone agree with me?"

Everyone on the board had substantial holdings in the bank and no one wanted to see their investment falter. They unanimously agreed to replace Ben. Don then asked who in the room would like to submit their name for chairman. After a pregnant silence, Sid Wyse said, "Don, you have taken the initiative to call this meeting and recommend replacing Rusk, why don't you take over as chairman?"

Don responded, "Sid, I do appreciate your confidence, but I'm trying to retire, not oversee a bank." And Sid retorted, "You have the most at stake here, you have the time, and right now we need you. After all, it is an interim position until this mess blows over. Then we can formally restructure."

After the board named Don Davino chairman by acclamation, he brought up the next order of business. "You all know that Ben had named Whit Cogswell CEO of the bank, but you also know he was not much more than a figurehead. Ben really called all the shots and made every key decision. I think we should give Whit a vote of confidence, give him our support, and let him have a chance to prove himself. I think he will step up to the plate and prove he is worthy of the position. He has a good team with extensive experience, and his skill is getting collaboration from people around him. I will personally advise him to work closely with the ELT. But if he doesn't measure up, then we replace him. Any comments?"

Before anyone had a chance to concur, Linda Honeycheck, the corporate counsel spoke up, "Wait a minute, Don. Cogswell has no real life experience in this role. Why would we support him, when we have a seasoned banker in John Youngman? He was passed over for the position because your family's clout pushed Ben to appoint Whit. It wasn't his skills, it was about appeasing you and protecting the flow of banking business your family represents."

Don fumed, but held his temper. "First of all Youngman is an old school has-been. He hasn't had an original idea in at least 20 years. You should have witnessed the contrast between his lame strategy at the ELT meeting yesterday and Whit's quick decision-making.

"And how do you know Ben didn't see something in Cogswell? Have you ever even had a meeting with Whit? I think it would be a mistake to make a change of the CEO position at this critical time. "We need to give Whit a chance to succeed or fail, and we need to monitor that trend very closely. I am recommending that we increase our board meetings to once a month for at least the next six months, and we have Whit attend and report at every meeting. This way we either develop a comfort level with him or recognize that he may be in over his head. Any objections?"

After getting approval for Whit's continuance, Don brought the board up to speed on the multi-faceted public relations and lobbying plan, citing its importance. He had Shawn waiting in his office to be summoned to the meeting and outline the overall vision of the PR program.

Shawn hadn't had time to prepare a PowerPoint presentation, but he spoke with authority and touched on the salient points. The overarching theme of the communication was that the bank was not being charged with any wrongdoing. This was strictly a personal action between the Justice Department and former chairman Ben Rusk. The message to their corporate clients would be that no changes were planned in the way the bank did business. Their loans, lines of credit and other services would continue without interruption. The communications program would also let the depositors know that their money was safe as the bank's financial position was extremely strong. And most important, the message would keep the legislators and regulators calm. In order to support that statement, he planned to publish an abbreviated balance sheet in the press to show the bank's financial strength. A few of the board members asked Shawn some questions, which he deftly handled.

With everyone satisfied that they had a sound plan, Don thanked the directors and asked for a motion to adjourn.

Chapter

55

It was Monday night, the scheduled evening for Cogswell's weekly card game with all his fraternity friends that lived in the area. The guys rotated locations to each other's houses, so about once every two months they held the game at Whit's place.

Lucille despised the games, but it was about the only social activity that he participated in, with the exception of his weekend tennis. She really disliked all Whit's friends from college. In her opinion, they were all socialite-wannabes that were so full of themselves that they expressed no interest in anyone else, particularly someone who wasn't a WASP. She also suspected that the only reason they included him was because of his position at the bank.

Whenever it was his turn to host, they expected her to have a full supply of beer and booze on hand, plus lots of hot and cold snacks to munch on all evening. They often played well into the early hours of the morning. And they left a mess of the den including the stale cigar and beer odor. She frequently went to her mother's and stayed overnight on these occasions.

Whit never told her that the games were high stakes with his losses often in the hundreds of dollars, and sometimes as much as several hundred, because he wasn't very good at cards. For him it was all about the social connection.

Chapter  56

Following the board meeting, Don Davino called Woodrow Horvath and advised him that Ben Rusk was voted off the board. Knowing the board had no choice, Horvath accepted the news recognizing that Rusk would be apoplectic over the turn of events. He knew Ben was still in denial over the entire episode, and was hanging on to the fantasy that it would eventually blow over with minimum personal damage.

Horvath had had a meeting that morning with Pippinger, who was not budging on his position regarding Ben Rusk. He advised Horvath that if Rusk did not turn himself in within the next week, he would be considered a fugitive. And that would only add to the charges piling up against him. He also let Horvath know that he had frozen all of Rusk's known bank accounts, cancelled his credit cards, and was monitoring all activity at StarTrust. Horvath said that he would get Rusk to return to the country and turn himself in. He also asked Pippinger to provide him a copy of all material given to him by Rothenberg's wife, plus any other evidence that he had accumulated.

Dreading the conversation he would have with Ben, he postponed it while he assembled a team of the best trial attorneys and investigators from the vast staff that comprised his firm.

At last he called Rusk and filled him in on all the news that wasn't available on the Internet or TV. Ben was devastated. He just couldn't believe that he could be brought down by a vindictive, ditsy wife. How could they throw him out of his bank, the bank he founded and built into an empire? The same bank that was now making millionaires out of these executives that were throwing him under the bus.

His answer was a definitive no. There was no way he was coming back now. He was not giving up his bank. And he was not turning himself in to the Feds. He was going to make it right. He had too many important connections and too many favors he could call in. He would go to the White House if necessary to get this trivial investigation squashed.

Expecting that Rusk's reaction would be along those lines, he said, "Ben, you are radioactive. No one is going to help you. They can't afford to be connected to you right now. So make your calls, and when you don't get a response, call me back and let's start planning your defense. I've already begun to assemble your team and we're working on our strategy to defend you. And keep in mind if you don't come back right away, you'll be declared a fugitive. And at that point, I can no longer harbor you at my private cay."

That last comment struck the chord that convinced Rusk of his hopeless position. He had no access to funds, either cash or credit cards, and now no place to stay. And being on the small island all by himself had only intensified his depression. He also knew that Horvath was right. No one, not even his closest allies would help him under these circumstances. This left him only one choice, and that was to return home and turn himself in. He reluctantly told Woody to send the yacht to pick him up the following day.

When Ben hung up, the realization caught up to him, and he was now fully convinced that his empire was lost. His life's work to build a banking juggernaut was now being taken away from him. It was final.

That night, he walked the small beach on the cay, drinking from a bottle of scotch. When the bottle was empty, he tossed it into the Atlantic, and had thoughts of following it into the water. It was the first time he had experienced serious depression, and was not equipped to deal with it. When he was waist high in the incoming tide, a rogue wave knocked him backwards, driving him back to the shallow ebb. He lay there on his stomach, sobbing for nearly an hour. When the waves began to roll over his head, it brought him back to reality. The water not only had a sobering effect on his consciousness, but also on his psyche. He finally dragged himself out of the shivering cold water and back to the house.

Ben spent the next few hours searching for a solution from this disaster. And as dawn was breaking, a plan emerged and he figured out what he had to do.

Chapter
57

Laura sat in her office, almost giddy. A month ago she was facing financial ruin with her agency about to collapse. The landlord was threatening to both evict her and to sue her personally for default on her rent payments. All she could think about was losing their house due to the loan and lease guarantees. And then she would have had to let go the last few staffers, her most loyal and trusted employees. Terminating people was a gut-wrenching experience, and doing it without cause on their part, always left her grief-stricken. It was easily the most difficult part of running any business. And no matter how many times she had to terminate an employee, it never got easier.

Suddenly, in a short period of time she had projects from the bank that would run into the millions. She started contemplating hiring back a few employees that she had laid off.

She called Shawn and said, "It's Friday night and we haven't had a dinner date in months. Let's have a quiet, romantic dinner. I will make a reservation at LeJardin in Edgewater, and you can meet me there at seven."

Laura arrived first, and took a booth seat that faced the front. She always liked to have a view of a restaurant's activities. When Shawn came in, she could see the difference in him. The energy was back, and the stress was gone. Before he sat across from her, he slid in alongside her, gave her a hug and a tender kiss.

"Laura, I finally feel like I'm being productive. Up until now I have hated this job, and I probably would have quit, except it has been our only source of income. As you know I thrive on action, and there has been none since I took the position at StarTrust. All of the other executives and managers seem content just sitting around doing nothing, or creating projects that are totally unproductive. They spend their days planning their next backstabbing tactic, kissing up to their bosses, and counting the days until retirement. I thought this only happened in the government, but corporate America is just as bad.

"With these new challenges, I am so energized. I can't wait to get to the office in the morning."

When the wine arrived, Shawn made a toast, "Laura my love. I am so proud of you. You kept the agency afloat under extremely difficult circumstances, and now, hopefully, we'll be able to breathe a little easier."

Laura couldn't speak as she was trying to contain the tears that started trickling from the corners of her eyes. Finally, she spoke, "I love you Shawn. I think it was your confidence in me that made me stay focused all through these excruciating times. I have never undergone so much stress. This experience has been so painful, that I really didn't think I could do it."

"Over the next few months you will be getting an overwhelming amount of work from the bank. And through it all StarTrust will become stronger, as will Image Concepts. And that should help relieve your stress. At the first opportunity, we'll take a small vacation to some quiet island destination and recharge our batteries."

Chapter 58

Whitney was surprised when he got the letter from the alumni association inviting him to the ten-year reunion banquet. Although he was in touch with a few of his college friends, mostly from the tony cities in Connecticut and the few frat brothers from the New York area, he never bothered with the association. In fact, he didn't even respond to the five-year invitation. At the time he was in a middle management job that his father had arranged and didn't want his friends to know about his lack of success.

But this year was different. He was the CEO of a large regional bank, and he would parade his beautiful wife at the event for his envious classmates.

When he told Lucille that they were going to the gala, she objected. "Why do we want to waste our time at a stifling event like that? For that kind of money, you can take me into New York for dinner at the Waldorf. And better yet, we could get a room and stay over for the weekend. We'd have to get a hotel room if we went to New Haven for the banquet. So why not spend the money on something that we could find memorable."

"No. Lucille. We are going. This is imperative. A lot of the graduates have gone on to important jobs, and this could be good for business. I want you to buy a new dress so you can look your stunning best."

As was expected, the banquet turned out to be a total bore, particularly for Lucille. All of Whit's college friends were afflicted with Larchmont Lockjaw, making them difficult to understand with their affected speech pattern. And none of them had anything interesting to say. They spoke about making partner at their law firms, their self-important positions in corporate America, and drivel about their country clubs. But Whit was ecstatic, being able to boast about his triumphs at StarTrust and his ascension to CEO. And he did notice the guys' approving glances at Lucille who looked magnificent.

When they drove home on Sunday afternoon, following brunch with a few of the couples from the party, Whit couldn't stop talking about how much bank business this weekend was going to generate. Lucille sat in the car thinking that the other women she met all had that vacuous look in their eyes that was no-doubt caused by their dull existence. She related to that look, seeing herself trapped in the same environment by her marriage to a self-centered egomaniac.

Chapter

59

Early Tuesday morning, John Youngman stopped by Dee Dee's office and invited her to dinner as promised for the following night. She suggested the Taj Mahal in Jersey City. John was unfamiliar with the restaurant, so Dee Dee called ahead and reserved a quiet booth in the back of the restaurant. She was excited about the prospects of a romance with John, if she could only get him to focus on her rather than himself. Of course, he was married, and she knew nothing about the strength of their marriage. But she was getting way ahead of herself.

The exotic setting got John excited, as his choice of restaurants didn't go much past noisy steak houses. He didn't know what to order, so he left it all to Dee Dee. She ordered a few appetizers and a bottle of wine, followed by a couple of the house specials.

Early in the conversation, he let her know that his wife was on Long Beach Island, visiting her sister in Loveladies. When they had finished their dinner and the wine, Dee Dee ordered two Yamazaki 18-year old whiskeys. They went down too quickly, and John suggested a second round. Emboldened by the alcohol, he started running his hand up and down her ample thigh. He was delighted when she did not object.

After he paid the bill, she suggested they go back to her place for coffee. "He responded, "I'll come by for a drink, but I never have coffee at night."

As soon as she closed the door to her condo, he started kissing and groping her. His breath was so bad, that she thought she'd throw up if he didn't stop. She said to herself, *"Doesn't he ever floss his teeth?"* After a few minutes of this heavy petting, she gently pushed him back and said, "John, you have a wonderful tongue. Let's get undressed and you can kiss me someplace else with that tantalizing instrument."

With that comment, John nearly burst his pipe. Within minutes, they were both naked on her bed, with his head between her thighs. She looked down at herself and noticed that the dieting and her work at the fitness center were showing results. She felt like she was looking better than she had in years. But those thoughts were pushed aside as John brought her to orgasm. After that, she climbed on top of him with her huge breasts dangling in his face. She gently inserted him into herself without causing an explosion, and rode the stiff pony for the few seconds it took until he came. She rolled off him, hoping for a short break and a rematch, but he fell asleep almost immediately.

After about an hour, he woke up to find Dee Dee snoring gently. He quietly got dressed, tiptoed out of the apartment, and rushed home, just in case his wife called to check up on him.

The next morning, Dee Dee got to the office at seven and quickly wrote a note on a sheet of display board in large bold type with a black marker.

WHAT THE FUCK HAPPENED TO YOU LAST NIGHT?

She placed the note right in the middle of Youngman's desk for anyone walking by to see.

Two hours later, a flustered John Youngman was standing in front of her desk. She looked up and asked, "What do you have to say for yourself, John? I gave you my body. You take it and then run off like a thief in the night. How do you think that makes me feel? Was it that bad?"

"I, I, I'm sorry, Dee Dee. When I woke up, you were sleeping so peacefully, I didn't want to disturb you. But please believe me. It was fabulous. I can't wait to have sex like that again."

Well that really set her off. "It'll be a cold day in hell before you get anywhere near me again. Now get the hell out of here, I'm busy."

"But I wanted to meet with Whit to discuss my ideas."

"I'll try to get you on his calendar. Now leave. I have work to do."

Reflecting on his comments after he left, she recognized that her idea of a relationship with John was an ill-advised fantasy. Like all the other promiscuous married men, he just wanted sex. And that put her in a funk the rest of the day.

Chapter

60

Later that morning, Serena McCormack came in and sat down at Dee Dee's desk. Noticing her dark mood. "Dee Dee," she said, "You look very depressed. What's wrong?"

"I had a terrible letdown with what I thought could be a promising date, but I really don't want to talk about it."

"I'm truly sorry about that. You really deserve someone who will appreciate your warm and caring qualities. Look, we haven't spent any time together, and as the only two women on this floor, not counting the secretarial pool, we should get closer. Let me take you to lunch today."

Dee Dee immediately thought about Serena's concern, and wondered why she could never find a man that exhibited those feelings. "I like that idea, Serena. Without Ben here, I think all the male baboons are starting to become agitated."

They went to lunch at a small restaurant on Washington Street and both ordered salads. After some small talk about each other's backgrounds, Serena commented, "Dee Dee, I want you to help me get closer to Whit. He's in for a difficult time over the next few months, and I can keep him from making any fatal mistakes. Please let him know that I can be trusted, and to give me some time to discuss the politics of the executive suite." Dee Dee replied, "That would be helpful.

I'll talk to him and get it set up."

As Serena was paying the check, Dee Dee asked, "Serena, I could use some advice from you, as well. I want to become more active in the dating scene, and I realize I have to update my wardrobe. One area that is really lacking is my choice of undergarments. I need to pick out some new lingerie that flatters me and hides the flaws. Could you help me with that?"

After lunch, they walked to an exclusive women's apparel shop and Serena selected the sexiest ensemble, which was also the priciest in the department.

When they went up to the register to pay, Dee Dee exclaimed, "Oh no. They don't take American Express and that's the only card I have with me. I'll have to get some cash and come back."

Reaching in her purse, Serena responded, "Don't be silly. I'll pay for it. It's not a problem." Stammering Dee Dee said, "But you just paid for lunch. I can't let you do this as well. It's way too expensive. I'll pay you back when we get to the office." "It's OK, Dee Dee. Trust me. It will be well worth it. You are going to make some guy drop dead when he sees you in this outfit." And with a little giggle, "It is so seductive, I wouldn't mind seeing you in it myself."

Chapter

61

After returning to New Jersey from the cay in the Bahamas, a contrite Ben Rusk, accompanied by his attorney, Woodrow Horvath, arrived at the US Attorney's office on Broad Street in Newark, and turned himself in to the Federal Prosecutor, James Pippinger. He was read his rights, and then arraigned and booked.

Ed Rothenberg's actions on the other hand, were completely different. The day before he was scheduled to surrender, he attempted to board a flight to the Cayman Islands using an assumed name and passport. FBI agents intercepted him at the gate in JFK Airport and escorted him away in handcuffs. Unnoticed by the agents was an attractive woman wearing sunglasses, sitting alone in the far corner of the gate area. When she saw the arrest, she waited until after the area cleared, then got up, dropped her boarding pass in the trash and left the airport.

After his arraignment, Rothenberg claimed his innocence, and refused to cooperate with James Pippinger. He would not testify against Rusk and any other people that provided illicit funds to his campaign. This tactic played into Ben's plan to become a key witness against Rothenberg. He not only was able to provide evidence of his bribery schemes with the senator, but he had knowledge about many of the illicit campaign finance deals that were funded by other benefactors.

As a result of the extensive network of bribery and other deals, plus his flight attempt and the myriad of other charges filed against him, Ed Rothenberg was convicted on multiple counts of bribery, extortion, mail fraud, income tax evasion and securities fraud. He was sentenced to 20 years in prison.

In consideration of his cooperation with James Pippinger's office, and his sincere showing of remorse, Ben Rusk was given a five-year sentence, to be served at the Federal Correction Institution, a medium security facility in Fairton, NJ.

Chapter  62

With a beaming Dee Dee sitting next to him, Donny Davino sat across from Whit in the conference room of the bank's executive suite. He was clean-shaven, and wore a tailored suit and expensive Italian leather shoes. She wrinkled her nose at his overpowering fragrance, noting that she would have to coach him about that. But the rest of the look was a real improvement.

Donny had a bold plan that he came to present to Whit, but first he wanted to share his financial statement with him. The real estate investment trust had been remarkably successful. Donny had an uncanny knack for picking winners from the scrap heap. In the short period since its launch, the portfolio had more than doubled in value and was trending even higher than that.

When he was convinced that Whitney was duly impressed, he said, "Whit, I got a killer idea that's going to make this statement look like chump change. We own all the original Dizzy Don's stores that we lease to Sid. I've been scoping out all the other stores that he had before the merger, plus the new locations that he has since opened. I made a list of the owners of every property where he has an outlet, and I had Randy Eigen quietly check out the possibility of acquiring each one of them. I have an idea how I can get them below market, but I can't share all the details with you right now. For this gig to work, I gotta do every deal at the same time. If word get out that I'm buying, the price goes nuts.

"We're in a good cash position right now but we're still going to need boodles of dough to pull this off. Take a look at this cash flow spreadsheet, and you can see, we can easily cover the payments."

Whit was impressed with Donny, both with his incredible success to date and his bold plan. This staged series of acquisitions would cumulatively represent the largest loan in the bank's history. However, since each was an individual deal, technically it became a series of medium-size mortgages, which he could approve. He would have Tom Mitchell do the grunt work and process all the documentation. But he wanted to grab the glory himself. So he would tell Tom that he would sign off on all the deals. "He said, "Donny, this is brilliant. I want to do this deal, but I must follow protocol. The Executive Leadership Team and the Board are looking over my shoulder, and the sharks are waiting for me to make a misstep. As soon as the commercial mortgage department processes the loans, I'll sign off, and you can get started with the acquisitions."

"Thanks, Whit. I was certain that you would see the value in these deals."

Dee Dee looked at Whit, winked and nodded.

Chapter 63

StarTrust's marketing and public relations campaign was now in full swing. Because the bank had not done very much communications in the public arena, the outreach was getting more than its share of attention. Its first article ever to appear in the Wall Street Journal highlighted the bank's rating and the impressive numbers it had achieved. Reserves were far more than required and profits in relation to its size were higher than the bigger international banks.

The consumer sales promotion program with discounted loan rates and free checking brought huge amounts of traffic to all the local branches. And on the commercial side, the results were similar. Businesses abhor the hassle of changing banks, even if the service is poor and the costs are high. Recognizing that, Shawn created an ad campaign that published testimonials of high-profile CEOs touting the amount of money they're saving in fees and interest after switching to StarTrust. And they boast that these savings are coupled with the great personal service that they have been receiving. The strategy of using business owners to deliver this message got other CEOs thinking about their banking relationships, and a trend began as companies started moving their accounts to the bank.

The surge in new business and the positive accolades expressed in social media completely changed the environment within the bank.

With renewed enthusiasm and rapidly improving morale, the entire staff stepped up their customer service and their visibility to their clients and depositors of every size as the bank enjoyed boom times like never before.

The campaign had a strong residual affect on the share price of the company's stock. Up until now it had languished, even dropping with the bad press surrounding Ben Rusk's indictment. But with the positive WSJ story and other glowing reports, the stock began to climb, recovering from its drop and reach new highs.

Shawn rightfully deserved all the praise he was now getting, plus the respect he earned from the Executive Leadership Team. Recognizing his skills and the contribution he was making to StarTrust's success, each of the other executives were now asking him to develop a campaign for their area of responsibility – home mortgages, trust services, personal loans, etc.

Whitney however, saw it differently. At each board meeting, when he had to make his monthly report, he took all the credit for the bank's success and rising share price. He even bragged how it was his marketing campaign that triggered the growth, pointing out his previous experience running Dizzy Don's advertising programs.

Chapter

64

When the call came into his cell phone from Reginald Nimmy, Whit was both surprised and delighted. "Whitney. It was great to see you at the alumni banquet. I marveled at how many of our gang are doing so well. You, a bank CEO, wow!"

"Hi Reggie, it is good to hear from you. And what are you up to?" Well, I was telling you about my business consultation firm at the event, and I just got a call from one of my key clients. The patent just came through on their new invention and they are looking for their next round of funding. They are considering investment or bank financing, and possibly a combination of both. This could be a made to order opportunity for you."

"Tell me about the invention, and how much are they looking for?" "The company is called Endless Energy and their system converts salt water to a fuel that burns extremely hot and efficiently. They need $2 million to manufacture 500 of the systems to fill a government contract they have with the Department of Defense. They would like to arrange a loan for this tranche, and a stock offering for the next round. The contract with the DOD is worth $18 million, a nine-times markup. Besides, the patent is easily worth 5 mil. That gives you $23 million as collateral. As you can see, the loan to equity ratio is extremely strong. And after processing the initial order of 500, the company is doing a private placement offer to raise another $20 million to expand production. If you want to put some of your own money in, the investment will have a very high multiplier."

"Rege, send me some documentation and I will get back to you quickly. It does sound exciting. Energy is always a strong sector, and clean energy will be even stronger."

When the package came in, Whitney shuffled through the paperwork with Dee Dee looking over his shoulder. He was impressed by the extensive patent documents, the lab reports, and the huge contract from the Department of Defense to purchase the units. Even she thought the deal looked very solid. Reflecting on his previous disaster with one of his classmates hawking what turned out to be a bogus deal with a new patent, he was very cautious. He told Dee Dee to have Linda Honeycheck review the documentation for both the patent and Department of Defense order. Whit wanted to be sure the patent was solid and the purchase order was firm. In the meantime, he ordered the lending team to process the files and deliver them to Honeycheck after they were prepared. He was not doing anything with this project unless Linda blessed every step.

Chapter

65

Serena stopped by Dee Dee's office and asked, "Were you able to set up a meeting for me with Whit?"

"Sorry Serena. Whit is working on a huge series of commercial mortgages that really has him tied up all week. I'll set something up over the next week or two, as soon as this big project is behind him." "By the way, have you had a date where you got to wear your new lingerie?"

"I did, but confusing is probably the best way to describe it." Although she was slightly embarrassed, she related the experience. "Gerry is good looking, athletic, and anal, but really thin. I think he's got a case of gone-ass. He is very focused on fitness, and his conversation was about the importance of organic foods, avoiding GMOs, gluten and red meat, limiting alcohol and on and on. Besides being bored to tears, I felt guilty about the Cosmo I was drinking and the dishes I ordered. His obsession made me self-conscious about my shape, even though I've lost so much weight and I'm better toned than ever. I didn't even invite him back to my condo after dinner, as I was afraid he would look at me and judge me because of my full figure. He wants to go out again, but I'm not sure what to do. I was feeling really sexy that night too, wearing those beautiful undergarments. I really wish you could have seen me in them." Dee Dee's expression had that naughty smirk.

The directness of her comment gave Serena a twinge in her chest. And with that Serena sat down and asked, "And he never got to see that gorgeous lingerie? What a waste. Tell you what. Why don't we have dinner at my place Sunday night? I'll prepare a light dinner and you can wear that new lingerie and model it for me. With my thin body, I appreciate a shapely woman. I have some sensual stuff in my wardrobe that I can show you. We can both lounge around, feeling sexy." Accepting the invite, Dee Dee replied, "That sounds like fun, certainly more fun than this latest date."

Chapter 66

Whit was staring at the pile of folders on his desk. Each one represented a retail site that his brother-in-law Donny wanted financed and each contained all the necessary applications, COs, appraisals, code approvals and more. The tenant lists looked good and the rental income easily covered the mortgage amounts with very positive cash flows. The two-foot high stack of paperwork had sat on his desk for a week now and he didn't know where to begin.

Dee Dee came in and chided him to get the process moving. This was a huge opportunity for the bank, and an important win for Whit. She had told him the day Donny brought in the deals to talk to Ron Phipps in the commercial lending department. He was a whiz at these real estate transactions. Whit had hesitated because he didn't even know how to explain this multi-mortgage project to Ron. He didn't want to let Dee Dee know how helpless he was, so he kept making excuses. But she saw through it and said, "I'll get Ron in here this morning and we'll both go over it with him."

When Phipps saw the extent of the deal he was amazed, but also apprehensive. Flipping through some of the folders, he remarked, "Whit, these transactions will require an enormous amount of capital, and I notice the purchase contracts are by many different entities. I take it you are blessing this series of loans."

It was Dee Dee who responded. "Ron, while Whit wants to go forward with them, he will only bless them after your due diligence and approval. The different entities that are purchasing the properties are all shells for my brother Donny's company. If property owners found out that his firm was acquiring all these retail sites, the prices would have increased substantially. So once the deals are consummated, the sites as a portfolio will be worth far more than the purchase prices. That in itself makes this a very attractive funding deal for StarTrust. Donny has always been a model commercial client for us. And while you may not have thought about it yet, the successful conclusion of these transactions could go a long way to securing maximum bonuses for the entire commercial real estate department."

Phipps left Whitney's office with an armload of folders and his head spinning with the potential of what he was carrying.

What Dee Dee failed to mention to Whit was that Donny had been circulating rumors through the commercial real estate brokers that Two Wyse Guys was overextended and may be encountering some financial issues in the near future. He was using Randy Eigen as his pipeline to getting the word into the field. She knew that when Phipps checked the appraisals he would see just how attractive the selling prices were.

Chapter  67

"Sid, this is Don Davino. We haven't spoken in a while. I wanted to meet you and get an update."

"What's the problem, Don? Haven't you been getting your payments on time?"

"Sid, your checks come in like clockwork, two weeks after the due date and the day before the penalty date. But I'm calling to share some good news with you. Let's have dinner in Fort Lee, because I hate to drive into the *facacta* city. We'll meet at Fanco's Metro. It's a BYOB storefront restaurant that serves excellent Italian food. And I'm bringing the wine, and buying dinner."

Later that week, Sid was sitting at a booth, when Don came in accompanied by his son Donny. After the usual back and forth insults that served as their greeting, Don got serious and said to Sid, "I brought Donny along and he has an important announcement. Donny, tell Sid what's about to happen."

"Sid, within the next few of weeks, I'm closing on all your buildings. I'm gonna be your new landlord."

This announcement caught Wyse by surprise and he got really nervous. "Are you serious? What's going on? Why are you moving on me like that? Are you trying to take over my stores?"

"I am in fact taking over the stores, but not the way you think. We view this strictly as a real estate deal, and we see a good investment in owning the properties where you have stores. In fact, we purchased a few locations that you may be interested in for some new locations. It's just a way for my REIT to ride on your success. Hey, we're paying you a compliment."

Sid was not assuaged. "Are you planning to raise my rents? I have leases on all those stores."

"Relax, Sid. We have no plans to raise your rent. In fact, we're actually going to improve the properties. You seem to have a knack for renting from the cheapest bastards in the industry, who never spend a nickel on their sites. Some of the parking lots look like war zones. We're going to do a lot of paving, upgrading the facades and whatever else it takes to make them prime retail locations. By the time we get done, we will have full occupancy in all the strip malls that you're in. And that will help increase your traffic."

At that point Don, Sr. added, "This will be a big win for you, Sid. Now let's enjoy dinner."

But Sid could not get past his paranoia. That's just the way he is wired. Instead of enjoying the meal and the camaraderie, he kept trying to figure out how this new development was going to hurt him. And he subconsciously kept feeling for his wallet.

Chapter 68

McCormack, Mitchell and Willis met at the Starbucks to find out about Serena's progress with Dee Dee. She reported that she was working on getting close to Dee Dee, but it was taking time to gain her trust. Without going into detail, Serena explained that they were meeting socially outside the office and sharing girl talk. The men were impatient and wanted to move quicker to get Whit out as CEO. They both felt that time was their enemy, citing the tremendous success of the marketing campaign. Another one or two wins, and there would be no viable reason to have him replaced by one of them. McCormack backed them off by saying, "Whit got lucky with Shawn's campaign. It's the first score he could claim since he's been with the bank. With his newfound self-confidence, he's bound to get reckless and screw up on the next project he undertakes."

Mitchell recognized why Serena wanted to move slowly as he felt time was on her side. He expected that the marketing campaign would substantially boost activity at the branches, making her the power going forward. So he decided to attack the unmentioned issue head-on. "Let's say Whit bombs on his next effort, or you convince him to step down, which of us will move to become the next CEO?"

Before Willis had a chance to open his mouth, McCormack pounced on the question. "I would be the obvious choice. The branches are already becoming hugely successful, and they are our most visible asset."

"Wait a minute," cried Bobby. Small Business is surging and is more profitable than the branches. And besides, I have seniority over you."

As the three of them got engaged in a heated discussion about which of them should be put up for the CEO's position, Hugo Sanchez walked into the Starbucks and saw them arguing. Guessing what was going on, he abruptly turned around and walked back out, hoping that they didn't notice him. The trio was so intent making their case, that none of them saw him come and go.

Sanchez went upstairs and walked into Todd Christopher's office to share what he surmised was happening at Starbucks. Todd agreed with Hugo, as he had been noticing the three VPs huddled in one of their offices on more than one occasion. While they both were on the Executive Leadership Team, they recognized that each of them was a notch below the others. Given this vulnerability, they agreed to watch each other's back.

When he got to his own office, Hugo thought about what his strategy should be going forward. The first step, he decided, was to get closer to Dee Dee. He would turn on his Latin charm to convince her that the International Banking Division was very important to the success of the bank, and his role was critical in growing that division.

Chapter  69

Serena's high-rise condo on Prospect Avenue in Hackensack had a stunning view across Bergen County to the beautiful sunset in the background. When Dee Dee arrived, Serena served her cocktails on the balcony. Dee Dee was wearing a long skirt and a low cut top that emphasized her ample cleavage. Her makeup was a little heavy, as was her perfume. Serena's blouse was transparent, revealing a lace bra beneath it and her skirt was tight and short which showed off her trim hips and long legs. She wore very little makeup, as her face didn't need it.

They sat in lounge chairs and sipped their Cosmos. After finishing a pitcher of them, they moved to the small dining area next to the living room for dinner. Serena had Bel Posto, across the street, prepare and deliver the appetizers and dinner. She served Meiomi Pinot Noir, which Dee Dee had never tried before. Accustomed to the heavy Chiantis, she was delighted by this lighter, but very tasty wine. After dinner, they finished the wine while sitting on the couch and snacking on Italian cookies.

After a while, they slouched back on the couch, silently enjoying the effects of the alcohol. Dee Dee reached over, began to stroke Serena's thigh and whispered. "You have such beautiful legs. My thighs are so heavy. I'd give anything to have legs like yours."

"And I'd give anything to have breasts like yours, Dee Dee. They are so voluptuous I just want to touch them. Men don't look at me they way they look at you."

"If you're referring to the Neanderthals in the office, you don't want that kind of attention. You have a beautiful, classy body, and a stunning face. Any man would want you."

The conversation and Dee Dee's stroking was getting Serena very turned on, but she didn't know how to take the next step. So she put her hand on her Dee Dee's arm and said, "Would it be alright if I touch you?"

Giggling, Dee Dee took Serena's hand from her arm and placed it on the exposed portion of her breast, saying, "You can touch me anywhere."

Serena responded with a muffled cry and began to gently massage Dee Dee's breasts. And with that, Dee Dee moved her hand up Serena's thigh and began to fondle her crotch. After a few minutes of petting, Dee Dee suggested that they go into the bedroom.

Standing next to the bed with hormones raging and inhibitions dulled by alcohol, they embraced gently at first, then with their bodies pressed together, they kissed deeply. After a few minutes, Dee Dee stepped back and began to unbutton Serena's blouse and then her skirt. In her lace bra and matching bikini briefs, she looked exquisite. Dee Dee stood there admiring this slender body, and gently running her hands up and down Serena's torso, but made no move to take off her own clothes.

Sensing her hesitation, Serena encouraged her by saying, "Let me take off your clothes so I can see your new lingerie and take in your lovely body." Dee Dee relinquished and let Serena slowly remove her clothes. The provocative undergarments certainly made her plump body look sexy and inviting, causing Serena to start touching her all over. They then lay on the bed kissing and exploring each other's bodies well into the night, sharing multiple orgasms.

Dee Dee slept over, but left early in the morning to go home, shower and change. She found the experience exhilarating and exciting, and easily as erotic as any man she had ever been with. Her curiosity and desire were pushing her to want to play out this role further, although she had strong reservations about Serena's ulterior motives. Driving home, she felt hung over and sick to her stomach. She emailed Whit that she had some personal errands to complete that morning and would be in late.

After about an hour's sleep, Serena lay in bed reliving every moment of the tryst. Even though she knew she was straight, she was thrilled by this lesbian experience. Dee Dee was so much more affectionate than the men she had been with. And she obviously wanted Serena to enjoy the maximum pleasure. "Would they ever do this again?" she wondered. Subconsciously she hoped they would, as she wanted to see where it would lead. She also thought it would benefit her goal of getting her audience with Cogswell.

Chapter 70

That morning at the ELT meeting, a gloating Whit made his announcement about financing the largest real estate transaction in the bank's history - all the malls and properties where Two Wyse Guys had leases. Expecting praise for this huge accomplishment, he was unprepared for the attack that came from everyone in the room. And without Dee Dee there to protect him, he was at their mercy.

The ELT members were shocked and outraged that he would negotiate and process a deal this big without bringing it to the team. Attempting to defend himself, he stammered that this was actually a series of relatively small mortgages for a client with an impeccable track record. And besides the commercial mortgage department had approved the loans.

John Youngman jumped on Whit, shouting, "Cogswell, you just don't get it. This is why we have an Executive Leadership Team, to discuss projects like this. Any individual deal would be routine, but collectively, this is a monster. While Donny Davino may have an unimpeachable history with StarTrust, he doesn't have unlimited credit. No client has ever been into us for this much money. Wait until the bank examiners see this. You're going to get skewered. I'd be shocked if they don't sanction us."

"I just delivered the most profitable piece of business the bank has ever seen, and all you can do is find fault with it? What is wrong with you people? We are here to make money."

Now it was Mitchell's turn to pour it on. "Whit, StarTrust is here to make money, but we're not a gambling hall. We have to stay within the banking rules and guidelines, and make our profit slow and steady. We can never afford to roll the dice, no matter how good the client's credit history is. And I'm speaking from personal experience. My bank went under because of a client with similar impeccable credit." With that comment the room went silent.

After a few minutes, Bobby Willis addressed Mitchell. "Tom, you'd better have your staff carefully review all of these deals to see if we're vulnerable for not following procedure to a tee. And make sure our funds are protected with the correct ratio of real estate values. I just hope somebody reviewed the leases on all the tenants of those retail outlets."

Of course Mitchell already knew all about the project. Phipps had given him a heads up after Whit handed off the packages. Tom told him to process them quietly and let him know if there were any problems with any of the deals. He wanted to use the lack of protocol to hammer Whit. But he wanted to do it at an ELT meeting rather than privately in his office.

Todd Christopher then spoke up and said, "Whit, we're going to have to report this to the Board right away. We all know they don't like to be blindsided, especially when it's this far outside our rules." Without thinking, Whit blurted out, "Don Davino already knows about the deals. He brought them to me." He had no idea how badly he had just thrown his father-in-law under the bus, just to save his sorry ass. Todd responded, "That's a huge problem right there, but you made it far worse by not following procedure."

Serena sat through the meeting without making a comment. While she wanted to land a few punches, she thought it best to remain silent before she got the opportunity to meet privately with Whit. Besides, she had a pounding headache from the combination of too much vodka, wine and adrenalin, with too little sleep.

Chapter

71

Dee Dee arrived at the office just before noon, but she still was not feeling well. Before she could get organized, Whit came running in and started to berate her. "Where the hell have you been? Of all the ELT meetings to miss, this is the one where I needed you most. Those ungrateful bastards tore me apart. I told them about Donny's real estate deals and everyone went berserk. They caught me by surprise and I did not know how to handle it."

Holding her head, Dee Dee said, "Whit, slow down and tell me exactly what happened. Otherwise I can't help you fix it."

Cogswell then proceeded to take her through the meeting step by step, as she sat there shaking her pained head. She asked a couple of questions about comments made by some of the attendees, and was surprised and pleased that Serena did not participate in the attack on Whit. At the end of his explanation, she shared her guidance, "Whitney, you should never boast about your own accomplishments. When someone else praises you, that's when you get the benefit of your action. And you never, never use your father-in-law as a reason for taking action. Now get out of my office and let me see how I can lessen the damage."

First, she called her uncle and told him what happened at ELT. Don was upset, but not really surprised by Whit's sophomoric handling of the project and his subsequent announcement about it. He told her to call Mitchell and explain that because of its size, he had blessed the deal and discussed it with a few of the board members. And that Whit should have brought Tom in on it right at the start rather than hand it off to one of Tom's staffers.

Mitchell was disappointed that this new twist was weakening his attack on Cogswell, but he didn't hesitate to complain to Dee Dee about Whit's inability to lead the bank. And he drove home the point using this meeting as an example.

After hours while Dee Dee was still in the office, Serena came in and sat down. "How are you feeling?" she said. "Today was a rough day, made worse by our all night escapade."

"Thank God I'm feeling better now, but it was the worst possible day to miss an ELT meeting. But it was worth all the pain to have enjoyed our time together."

"They crucified Whit at the meeting, but he deserved it. He should have never handled a deal like that on his own. At another bank he would be terminated. If he were my report, I would have fired him. And that points to the reason why I need to sit down with Whit. I can help him, so he doesn't make another blunder like that. Were you able to set up an appointment for me?"

"Serena, Whit will be spending all week undoing the damage from this fiasco. It will be next week at the soonest. I will talk to him, though."

Reaching across the desk, Serena touched Dee Dee's hand and asked, "And what about us? Can we get together again this week? I really want to be with you again."

"It's going to be a difficult week, but I'll let you know. And I want to see you again, as well."

When Serena left her office, Dee Dee sat there seething. Did Serena actually think she could help Whit or give him better advice than she was giving him? Does she really have Whit's best interests at heart? Was their "date" just a ploy to use Dee Dee to benefit her own agenda?

She really wanted to be with Serena again, but now there was an issue. In her heart, she wanted to touch Serena's body again, to feel that closeness and the intimacy, but now she was afraid of the emerging conflicts. She didn't know how to handle the relationship and it was all very troubling.

Chapter

72

The next morning Shawn DiPisa came into Dee Dee's office early, before the rest of the staff arrived. He had a plan he wanted to share with her. "Dee Dee, I have an idea that will overcome yesterday's bashing of Whit by the ELT. Now here's what I need you to do. Get to Ron Phipps and anyone else who worked on those contracts and make sure every one of them is rock-solid. Confirm that every lease and sub-lease is clean and there are no delinquent payments from any of the retail tenants. Confirm all that to me ASAP, and I'll turn this disaster into an opportunity for Whit. But in order to make this work, we've got to keep it under wraps."

"OK. I'll confirm the strength of the deals, but I'm sure they are all A-plus. Both Don and Donny were heavily involved with them. And I know after Phipps approved them, Linda Honeycheck reviewed all the paperwork. So, what's the next step? How are you going to work your magic?"

"One step at a time. I'm still working this out. I will have more information when you call me back."

Shawn wasn't even out the door when Dee Dee was on the phone summoning Phipps to her office with instructions to bring all the documentation on the contracts.

When Shawn got back to his office he called Laura and told her what he was thinking, and gave her the research assignment.

By 10 o'clock that morning, Dee Dee was convinced that the mortgage contracts were airtight. In just about every contract, either Two Wyse Guys or a national chain was the key tenant, and with very few exceptions all the smaller tenants were consistent with their rent payments. Phipps explained that since the appliance chain banked with StarTrust, he was able to review their financials. They were strong, and growing steadily. The other tenants benefitted from the traffic that Two Wyse Guys generated, and for the most part, they were solid as well. The few questionable tenants were so insignificant, that they had no impact on the decision to move forward with all the deals. She also confirmed with Honeycheck, that legally everything was in order.

Dee Dee was so excited that instead of calling, she ran down to Shawn's office. "Shawn, Ron Phipps thinks these deals are very solid. The tenant income, primarily from Two Wyse Guys is steady, and he thinks the properties are worth much more than the appraisals. Donny did an outstanding job negotiating these purchases. "So tell me the plan. I'm dying to know."

"Laura just called me back after she pitched a correspondent at the Wall Street Journal. He's going to interview Whit on landing one of the biggest real estate transactions of the year. The story will break Thursday, the same time we make the internal announcement and the press release hits the news media."

"Shawn, that's brilliant! That's going to shut down the attacks on Whitney." And with a smirk she added, "It's also going to seriously piss off some people in the executive suite."

Chapter

73

Before business hours on Thursday morning, an internal email blast informed all StarTrust employees about the massive real estate deal that Whitney had shepherded through the commercial loan department. The communication also noted the Wall Street Journal story that broke in that morning's edition.

Shawn read the interview and noted that it was short on individual praise for Cogswell, but it didn't disparage him either. The reporter actually wanted to do a video interview, but on orders from Shawn, that was turned down. The last thing Shawn wanted was a fumbling CEO tarnishing his credibility by incorrectly answering any of the tough questions that would certainly be asked.

With the exception of the ELT, everyone in the company felt pride in the rare national publicity garnered by the bank. By contrast, Mitchell was fuming, and he called Willis and McCormack to meet for drinks after work to talk about this unexpected setback.

Bobby and Serena arrived at the same time to find Tom at the bar on his second vodka, poured in a rocks glass full of olives and ice. He wasted no time taking his frustration out on McCormack, "Serena, you were supposed to talk to Whit and get him to meet with the three of us. What the hell happened?"

"Hey, don't blame me for this turn of events. I'm working on

Dee Dee, but she guards Whit like a prison warden. I'm gaining her confidence, but it's not going to happen overnight. We'll probably get together again in the next few days, and I'll get to sit with Cogswell. But now it's going to be a lot harder to convince him that he can't run the bank and should step aside. We may have to wait until his next blunder."

Bobby Willis spoke up next and agreed with Serena. "We shouldn't have to wait long for his next misstep. He's a walking disaster. If Dee Dee weren't constantly covering his ass, he'd be toast by now. Maybe we should change our tactics. Serena, do you think you could become Dee Dee's best friend and convince her that Whit is holding back the bank from growing faster? Here's an idea I thought of this morning after I read the press story. We could create a new position, that of Chief Operating Officer. One of us could fill that role and actually run the bank. Whit would still be President/CEO and keep his fancy title, but would not have to deal with the daily grind of decision-making. Instead he would be given a new set of responsibilities. He would become the special ambassador of StarTrust, calling on our biggest clients and schmoozing them. It's about the only talent he has, and he'd probably like that. We could get Shawn to create a campaign around it, announcing Whit's expanded role in building a closer relationship with the bank's largest and most important customers. I think his ego would respond with joy over the new role, and the exposure from the publicity. What do you think?"

Both Mitchell and McCormack liked the idea, although they thought it was a long shot. Whit relished sitting on the throne in the corner office but he also wanted to make all the decisions. And it would take an earthquake to move him away from that responsibility.

After thinking about the suggestion for a few minutes, Serena agreed, saying, "Let me keep working on Dee Dee. We've found some common ground, and since we're both single, I'm helping her with the dating scene."

Willis interrupted her with the comment, "If she showed some more cleavage, guys would be all over her."

"Bobby, grow up. Dating is a lot more than flashing your girls at breast-fixated slugs like you. Give me a little more time and she and I will be best friends. We're almost there."

Chapter  74

Two or three times a week, Whitney stopped to get his Corvette washed at Luxury Auto Spa, on the way to the office. The blue convertible was his compromise with Lucille on which car he should buy. She convinced him that if he was going to be taken seriously at StarTrust, he couldn't park a Lamborghini or Maserati sports car in the bank's garage. And while the Vette was extremely expensive, it cost far less than the six-figure exotic sports cars. Whit came to really appreciate the luxury of this sleek roadster and he made sure it always looks its maximum best.

As one of the best customers at the auto spa, he became friendly with the owner Pablo Alvarez. Pablo liked to chat up the car with Whit, knowing it was his pride and joy. And Cogswell was always ready to talk to anyone who would listen. He told Alvarez that this Corvette came with a 5.7 liter, 350 horsepower, fuel-injected engine. He also mentioned that the color was called Electron Blue Metallic. And Whit loved to point out the message he had lettered across the back deck, between the taillights.

Blew By You!

One morning Pablo approached Whit to ask about banking services.

He explained that they were getting ready to open another car wash, but their bank did not have a branch anywhere near the new location. And location was important to them because they made night deposits of their receipts every evening, which usually included large amounts of cash. As it turned out, StarTrust had a branch only one block away. Whit said to Pablo, "Come to my office today and I'll have my assistant set up an account for you. I will also get you a reduced rate on all your cash deposit and checking account fees. And will you consider quietly detailing my car once a month in exchange?"

Alvarez was delighted. "No problem, Mr. Whit. I come after lunch, and you can be sure, we will take very good care of your car. And you tell your people that we will give them special treatment too."

When he got to the office, Whit told Dee Dee that Pablo Alvarez was coming in that afternoon to open a retail business account. And he wanted her to handle the paperwork.

"So why is he coming here at headquarters? Why doesn't he just go to a branch and open an account?"

"I offered him a small deal by lowering some of his fees. He also speaks broken English, and probably was reluctant to go to a branch, where we might not have someone who speaks Spanish. Pablo is also going to provide some extra services for my car. And I will see that he does the same for yours."

Dee Dee called Bobby Willis and explained to him about Whit's new car wash client. She asked him if anyone on his staff that spoke Spanish was available that afternoon to help open the account. Willis suggested Angela Cervino, one of his emerging stars who was loved by the Hispanic community, and gave Dee Dee her extension.

Chapter

75

Following the successful PR effort to publicize the commercial real estate deals, combined with the initial campaign for the bank branches, Shawn was becoming the rock star of the ELT. Everyone wanted to take advantage of his strategic thinking and productive campaigns. At the same time, Image Concepts was making record profits from all the diversified projects coming from the bank.

Not wanting to miss out, Todd Christopher came to Shawn DiPisa's office and asked for help for his division. "Shawn, I need you to work your magic for the retail lending department. We have trouble competing with credit unions on auto loans, and besides, most people finance through the car dealers thinking they're getting low interest rates. Because of that reality, we're not going to concentrate too much on that segment of the loan business. My real interest however, is selling residential mortgages. The housing market is on fire and we're not getting anywhere near our share of the business. National lenders like Countrywide and Wachovia are saturating the media with ads and siphoning off a hugely disproportionate share of the business. Our rates are very competitive with theirs, so with some promotional support we can up our share of the business. I have some ideas, but I need a budget allocation to help market home mortgages."

"What do you have in mind, Todd? I'm sure we can help you with your division's product line."

"I've been doing a lot of networking and have made some high level contacts at a few of the larger real estate firms. There's a realtor's event in Atlantic City in a few months, and I want to have a presence at that conference. I'd like to sponsor the golf outing and maybe the banquet. By supporting some of the activities, I can get a few perks, like presenting a breakout seminar on mortgage lending or possibly be one of the speakers at their educational sessions. I am already qualified to teach continuing education classes, and these realtors need to be earning credits on an ongoing basis.

"The other effort I want to undertake, is some advertising directly to the homebuyers. The combination of awareness and referrals will help us compete for much more business."

"Todd, this is all doable. I'll put together a media plan to determine an advertising budget. How much do you need for the convention?"
"If you can set aside about $50,000, every attendee will know about StarTrust. The ad spending will obviously be a much larger amount, but I'm looking to grow the residential mortgage business by a half billion to a billion dollars a year."

"Great. We'll test market a campaign and spend a couple of hundred thousand dollars. If that works, we'll expand it throughout our entire market. In addition, we can do an in-house campaign for all the branch staff with a rewards program for referrals they generate.

Christopher walked back to his office feeling elated. He knew Shawn would put together a program that would make his department a huge profit center for the bank. And that would raise his stature on the ELT.

Shawn called Laura and explained his ideas for the mortgage campaign. He asked her to have her creative team come up with some graphic design concepts. His theme was fast turnaround. Most banks took up to a month to process a mortgage application, but StarTrust was going to promise a two-week completion. He wanted signage for the branches, ads in the real estate section of the newspapers, and radio spots during the day.

Chapter

76

At Dee Dee's suggestion, she and Serena met for drinks after work that Friday. McCormack was disappointed as she wanted to have Dee Dee over to her place again. She also sensed a slight coolness in her demeanor. The bar they chose was very loud. The young crowd was already starting to celebrate the weekend.

Dee Dee got right into what was on her mind. "Serena, I really like you, but I'm concerned that you are trying to use me to get to Whitney. Like everyone else, you really don't understand him. He's sensitive and shy, so he comes off as aloof and out of his league as CEO. It's my job to keep the vultures away from him so he can do his job without all the distractions from the executives that have no respect for him."

"But Dee Dee, he doesn't have the experience that the rest of us have, and because of that he's prone to make more mistakes. We're concerned for the sake of the bank.

"And I'll be honest, I was trying to get close to you, hoping that you will help me get access to Whit. But our relationship has become more than that. I've dated lots of men and have never felt the way I did when I was with you. I'm hoping you feel the same because I want to see where this goes. And regarding Whit, why can't we work together to make him more successful?"

"Serena, I'm not sure how to handle these personal feelings either, but I do enjoy being with you. You make me feel like a woman, and very few men have been able to do that. But I'm not sure what to do about Whit. So let's take it a step at a time, slow and easy."

After their second Cosmos, they began to get hoarse from talking over the crowd noise. So Dee Dee decided to ask Serena over to her place.

When they got there, Dee Dee poured them each a glass of Nonino Grappa. Serena tasted it and was surprised by its smoothness and unique taste. They sat in the living room, downed the first glass and sipped the second. There was still a little awkwardness between them, so Dee Dee stood up, took Serena by the hand and said, "Let's go to the bedroom." And as they were stripping off their clothes, Dee Dee suggested that they get into the shower together. Her oversize bathroom had a huge shower with multiple spray heads. With only the light from the bedroom, the shower provided a surreal sensation. They playfully soaped and massaged each other's bodies, washing them down. After toweling each other dry, they got into bed, each feeling invigorated and very lusty. The sex this time was far more aggressive, with Dee Dee taking the lead.

In the morning, Dee Dee made a light breakfast of toasted Italian bread with homemade preserves, and cappuccino. They sat around in a couple of nightgowns from Dee Dee's closet. After a while, they went back into the bedroom, enjoyed more sex, and after showers, Serena left for home.

When she was alone, Dee Dee thought about the relationship that was developing with Serena. She was conflicted about getting too close to her because she knew that she could not allow Serena to influence Whitney. And yet she was fascinated by the pleasure that was coming from being with her. But even the personal liaison was troubling her. Did she want a long-term relationship with another woman? Could she see herself in a lesbian liaison? She would have to see where it led, if anywhere.

Chapter

77

On Monday morning an excited Hugo Sanchez was standing in front of Dee Dee's desk and said to her, "I've got to see Whit. I have a tremendous opportunity that the bank can exploit. And I'm talking tens of millions of dollars in profit." Sanchez was Cuban-born with handsome Latin looks and a permanent smile. He was slightly short, but very athletic and had the graceful moves of a dancer. Before coming to the bank he was the South American representative of a multi-national manufacturer, and he was fluent in several languages.

"Hugo, I can sense your enthusiasm, so you must be onto something big. Whitney is buried with some major issues, and the auditors are in this week. I am also backed up, so why don't we meet over lunch and you can tell me about your plan? And I'll see if I can get Whit interested and have him set some time aside for you."

"Then let's do it today, as this deal is hot. Are you free?"

In a tactical move to create the right mood, Sanchez picked a Cuban restaurant called, La Isla. After they ordered, Hugo gave Dee Dee a brief description of his previous career. He had spent most of his adult life working for a European conglomerate that bought raw materials and sold refined composites for manufacturing processes to companies throughout the world. Hugo's sales territory was Central and South America. It was a big job with lots of responsibility, but like most

European companies, compensation was below market, and corporate advancement was reserved for the European-born insiders. In frustration, he ultimately left, and after meeting Ben Rusk at a political fund raiser, was offered a position with his bank.

As they completed their lunch, Hugo explained his deal. He had had dinner with a few former associates over the weekend, and they were all connected to major corporations throughout The Caribbean and South America. Nearly all of the southern hemisphere was booming, but there was a shortage of funding to fuel the growth. The largest international banks in the world were doing huge bond deals with the governments of these countries, as well as with the major national corporations like Petrobras, Pemex, Copec Energy, and others. That left the hundreds of very large companies that were severely underserved with their financing requirements.

"In my last career, selling to these Central and South American companies, cash flow was always an issue. And with the expanding economy, they are in dire need of funding. The guys I had dinner with the other night, using their connections have formed a consulting firm to offer financial aid and other solutions to their company contacts in all these countries. And because of my long-term relationship with them, they came to me first to see if StarTrust would like to be a key financial resource.

"With the billions of dollars flowing into South America from the world's banks, these companies will grow exponentially. Some of them are actually former clients from my previous career. It's a low-risk venture that we can get into at the early stage. What do you think?"

"Hugo, your enthusiasm alone has aroused my interest. Let me think about how to approach it with Whit, but before I do that, I have lots more questions. I don't have to tell you all the scrutiny Whitney is undergoing. So I want to be extremely comfortable that any deal that comes across his desk is rock solid. As I said this morning, my days are choked, so can we meet after hours for drinks or dinner and get deeper into the details?"

"Sure. I'm free tomorrow evening. I will pull together some documentation that we can review. And I'll book dinner at a quiet restaurant where we can talk."

Chapter 78

Angelo Davino came into StarTrust's executive suite and went to Dee Dee's office. He greeted her with a kiss on the cheek and, "Hiya sweetheart. I've got to see Whit about a business loan. Is he busy?"

"Angelo, you can't just walk in here and expect to see the CEO of a large bank, even if he is your brother-in-law. He is buried. How can I help you?"

"Now that Donny owns all those malls, he gave me this ginormous contract to handle the maintenance of every one. That involves sweeping, striping, painting, snow plowing, pavement repair and maintenance, you name it. With over 100 malls, I need to buy all this heavy equipment, like trucks, street sweepers, loaders and stuff. And I gotta hire a bunch of guys that can run the stuff."

"OK. So how much do you need? Did you bring in any paperwork?"

"Well no, I don't know what papers are necessary. I need nearly $3 million dollars for equipment alone, plus a line of credit to manage the payments."

"Angelo, for that kind of money, you'll need copies of your contract with Donny's company, a list of equipment with quotes from dealers, your financial statements and a business plan."

"Dee Dee, I aint got none of that. Donny hasn't even finished the contract yet, but I gotta get going on some of the work. And besides,

I want to walk into the dealers with money in hand, so I can negotiate the best deals. These trucks and stuff cost big bucks. So can Whit sign off on the loan, or should I go to my pop?"

"Your dad can't process a loan. He's the board chairman. You get as much of your paperwork ready as you can. Call your accountant. He can help you, and get the contract from Donny right away. I'll see if Whit can arrange some interim financing to help you get started."

Late that afternoon, Dee Dee went into Whit's office with a loan application for $250,000 for Angelo's company. She said to Whit, "Sign off on this loan, so Angelo can buy some trucks and other equipment. This is for his new maintenance contract to service all Donny's properties. When he gets his paperwork together, he'll be looking for about an additional $3 million for all the rest of the equipment, plus a line of credit."

Cogswell scanned the app and initialed it. Dee Dee took it back and dropped it off to the loan-processing department with instructions to deposit the funds in Angelo's business account once the paperwork was completed. She then emailed Tom Mitchell and gave him a heads-up on the loan with details to follow.

Chapter 79

Dee Dee arrived at the restaurant about 10 minutes after Sanchez. Before she arrived, she removed the cardigan she was wearing at the office and left it in her car. The sweater had covered the low neckline of her blouse, and now the ample cleft between her breasts was inviting everyone to take a look.

Hugo was sipping a mojito and when he saw all that flesh as Dee Dee leaned into the booth and sat down, he nearly choked on his drink. Recovering from getting caught staring at her chest, he said, "They make a great mojito here. Would you like one?"

Knowing the blouse accomplished its mission and had him off kilter, she responded, "I've never had one, but it looks healthy."

Over drinks they reviewed the details of Hugo's concept. He had a list of prospective companies and the amount of money they were looking to raise. His documentation included current sales, future projections, company financial ratings, maturity dates and rates, and anticipated revenue. The profit estimates were extraordinary. Hugo's plan was very impressive and Dee Dee was becoming very excited about the prospect of having this book of business at StarTrust.

With the business discussion completed and just before they ordered their third round and dinner, Dee Dee suggested, "Hugo, why don't we get out of here and go back to my place? My mother dropped off some lasagna today, and it's way too much for me."

With Sanchez constantly sneaking peeks at Dee Dee's boobs, it didn't take anything more than the dinner suggestion to agree to go to her condo.

While Dee Dee heated up the food, Hugo, who was already heated up, opened a bottle of wine. They chowed down the lasagna like two starving homeless people. And while Hugo loaded the dishes in the sink, Dee Dee came up behind him and starting rubbing her body against his. "Hugo, you are one sexy Cuban and I want you."

He turned around and said, "I've really got to get home, but there's no way I'm leaving here with this erection you've just created."
They quickly stripped and jumped into bed for a fast but hot sex romp. It didn't take long for him to bring her to orgasm before he had his.

Just as quickly, Sanchez washed up, got dressed and headed for home. He was a little surprised by Dee Dee's aggressiveness in inviting him back to her place, and then putting the move on him. His macho ego was only slightly bruised however, but quickly assuaged by his taking over the lead in the sex. Before being married he had prided himself as the Latin Lover with all the moves. He was convinced that their sexual encounter sealed the deal for her help in getting this program approved.

After Hugo left the condo, Dee Dee put on a housecoat and finished cleaning up the kitchen. She couldn't sleep, so she poured another glass of wine and sat on the couch, reflecting on the evening. The sex was good. Hugo certainly knew how to get her to come quickly with a sustained orgasm. But the overall experience left her feeling a little empty. As usual there was no warmth afterwards. Men just didn't understand that they came down from the euphoria far faster than women. And every woman wants to be held after sex in order to prolong the intimacy. So naturally she was disappointed, and sat there feeling lonely. She appeased her guilt with the knowledge that allowing these sexual encounters gave her control over Hugo and the other executives. She also knew that she was being used by him and the others to get her help with their approvals. But that was OK. She wanted to manage the process. And she felt this was an excellent opportunity for the bank. When she got the deal pushed through, it would be a positive reflection on Whitney. The board would praise him for his foresight.

Chapter 80

Serena spent a quiet Sunday by herself. She needed the solitude to evaluate her situation at the bank and think about her relationship with Dee Dee. She started the day taking a run at Overpeck Park, which boosted her metabolism. This would help her to think clearly. When she got back from the park, she got into the shower after letting the hot water steam up the entire bathroom. With the shower head set on massage pulse, she stood under the beating spray and the thoughts of her showering with Dee Dee came flooding back. After she toweled off, she lay naked on the bed, staring at the ceiling and trying to sort out these emotions. She kept saying to herself, *"I'm not a lesbian."* But the fact remained that she was smitten with Dee Dee. The intimacy was so much stronger than any man she had ever been with. And she was surprisingly comfortable with this woman-to-woman relationship.

The stronger conflict she grappled with was overcoming the challenge at the office. For her career to move forward, she had to overcome the blockade that kept Cogswell out of her reach. She was stymied by this irrational interference. But she had to assert herself with Dee Dee, and do it in a way that didn't damage their relationship. Tomorrow would be the day to set it straight.

Chapter

81

On Monday morning Dee Dee met briefly with Whit and told him that she was working with Hugo Sanchez on a huge series of loan deals with Central and South American-based companies. "I've checked out some of the documentation with Sanchez, and the deals are solid with very good margins. The total funding will grow to become a little over $1 billion. But they are all standalone deals with multiple companies from many different countries. You can counter-sign them when he has these files of paperwork and legal reviews complete."

Whit's comment to her explanation was, "Of course I want to sign off on any large deal. That is my job, with or without the loan officers. But I am concerned about going into such a large number of deals with international companies, particularly the people from the Southern Hemisphere. They tend to be so unrefined."

"Whitney, don't be prejudiced. This opportunity is the reason why Ben originally hired Sanchez. It was to build an international banking division. He has the expertise for these kinds of negotiations. He has worked the Central and South American markets for years. He really understands the mindset there. I have spent a lot of time on this and have a very high comfort level with this program."

After he reluctantly approved the concept, she called Hugo and told him to move forward with the project. He was ecstatic and couldn't believe she got approval to begin the due-diligence process that quickly. Attributing it to his self-aggrandized prowess in bed, he asked Dee Dee to have dinner with him again.

"Look Hugo, we had fun the other night, and maybe some time we'll do it again. But don't think for a minute that this will be a regular thing between us. You came to me with a very solid proposal, and I acted on it. Period."

"Oh, Dee Dee, please understand. I meant no disrespect. I just want to take you to dinner to thank you for your intercession."

"Let it go, Sanchez. I wasn't born yesterday."

About 1 pm, when the executive suite was nearly empty with just about everyone out to lunch, Serena came into Dee Dee's office. As soon as she sat down, she said, "Dee Dee, I've been thinking a lot about our situation, and we need to separate the business side from the personal. I have an agenda regarding the bank and I need your help to get us to the next level. I also have strong feelings for you and I want to nurture them outside our work relationship. We're both intelligent women and I'm confident that we can move forward on two separate tracks. Do you think you can do the same?"

"Serena, I have no problem with our personal relationship, but I have to draw the line on how we conduct business. I have a protocol to follow, as Whitney grants very few appointments. You and the other ELT members are pushing very hard to weaken his control and I can't allow that. I just can't be part of a power grab. None of you really understands Whitney nor appreciates the job he does. We have had very few glitches since he has taken over, despite how quickly StarTrust has grown. You need to talk to the others and make them back off. We will all be better for it. And then you and I can work on our relationship."

Serena left the office frustrated, as she has not been able to make Dee Dee realize Cogswell's shortcomings, or get past her blind trust and motherly protection. Walking back to her office she decided to back off on this tack, and keep getting closer to Dee Dee on a personal basis.

Chapter

82

As word got around about Luxury Auto Spa becoming a bank client, and that Dee Dee had VIP discount cards for the executives, they all began to use the facility. Tom Mitchell became a regular customer, and befriended Pablo's brother Hector who managed the new location nearer the bank's headquarters. Hector on occasion would provide Tom with a nickel bag of very high quality pot. After work one day, as he was on his way to meet Willis and McCormack for drinks and an update on progress with Cogswell, he stopped off for a car wash.

While he was waiting for his car to emerge from the tunnel, Hector came up to him and said, "Hey Meesta Tom, nice to see you. Come into office, I have gift for you." Hector took out a small vial of white powder and said to Tom, "This is very new drug. Just came in. Like cocaine, but is not addictive. Try one sniff. You like."

Mitchell took a small hit and immediately felt the euphoric buzz. When he entered the bar still feeling the effects of the drug and found McCormack and Willis already well into a conversation. Bobby was complaining about the absence of progress with Dee Dee, and Serena defended her efforts by saying, "Look Bobby, I have tried everything. I've schmoozed her, befriended her, bought her gifts, and even appealed to her protective stance with Whit. She's not going to budge, so I'm backing off. One of you can take your shot and see how your irresistible, cleavage-focused male charm will work."

Mitchell jumped into the fray and volunteered himself. "I can get to her. She's always flirting with me."

Serena laughed to herself, recognizing Tom's overinflated image of himself. And when Bobby agreed that Tom should make a go of it with Dee Dee, they settled down and enjoyed their drinks. After some small talk about the office, Mitchell shared his experience at the car wash. He told them about the sample hit he had that was so great that he bought a vial. He told them Hector sold it to him at an introductory price of only $50. He offered each of them a taste. Bobby was willing to try it, but Serena balked. "I don't put anything harmful in my body. I spend exorbitant prices on organic food, free-range chicken and wild caught fish. And you think I'd take a chance with some cocaine derivative made from an unknown source? You're both crazy."

When they came back from the men's room, the two of them were giddy. Bobby said, "I'm going to the car wash tomorrow and buy a bag. This is so much better than the weed, and much more convenient to use. And he said that it's not addictive? How can we be sure?"

Tom responded, "I've done coke once or twice, and this is different. But I can only go on Hector's statement. And he was pretty confident about his claim. I can tell you, after using it a few times, there is no compelling urge or constant need to take more."

Chapter  83

When Todd Christopher called Dee Dee and requested a meeting with Cogswell, she asked, "What is it about? Maybe I can help you."

"We just launched a marketing campaign to increase the home mortgage business, and it is working well. I want to bring Whit up to date on the progress, but I also want to discuss with him some ideas to make us more competitive."

"I don't have time to discuss it with you now. Are you available to meet at 12:30 today? Maybe we can have a working lunch in my office."

Dee Dee ordered some wraps and salads from the dining room, and Todd came in promptly at 12:30. As he sat down, she looked at him and realized that she had never really paid much attention to him. He was tall with a solid build, except for the bulge around his middle, and a good-looking face that always wore a mischievous smile. He made you feel like it was important to be around him, as he always seemed to be having fun.

Without touching his food, he jumped right in and began to tell her about the early success of the mortgage program. Applications were coming in from every corner of their service area, but Todd was convinced that they were barely touching the surface of the market. "We have to reach out to the small and mid-size developers that don't have their own mortgage companies, and also get to the realtors. Agents are at the point of sale and are in a position to refer huge volumes of business to us. We need to come up with some promotions to attract the real estate brokerages that can deliver their customers to StarTrust. And we should also be thinking about introducing a discounted interest rate so we can get ahead of the competition.

"I need to get approval from Whit to move ahead with all of these recommendations. He has to pass on the small introductory rate reduction, and although I already have the budget for the promotions, he's the one who has to approve any co-op marketing programs with the realtors. I brought along some reports to support my plans so Whit can review the entire program."

Scanning through the documents, Dee Dee was impressed with Christopher's presentation of the facts to support his suggestions. "Todd, let me study this material for a day or so. I know I'm going to have lots of questions, so let's plan to get together again later in the week. Maybe we can meet again for lunch. I just have no time during regular business hours for uninterrupted conversation."

Chapter

84

StarTrust's board meetings were held on the first Tuesday of each month. And this meant that Dee Dee spent most of the previous weekend preparing Whitney's board report and all day Tuesday prepping him on his presentation. It was an arduous task, and Cogswell never seemed to absorb enough of the process to do any of the work himself.

And so when the board secretary called on him, he listlessly handed out the copies of his report and highlighted the bullet-point items on the few slides he presented. Since the time he took over as CEO, there had been a slow, steady growth in just about all of the business sectors. This was in keeping with the bank's conservative posture. The last few months, however, the rate of increase in all categories began to grow at a faster pace, and so did the profits.

As with every meeting, Dee Dee sat at Whit's side and either prompted his responses to board member's questions or answered them herself. At the end of this month's report and Q&A, Don Davino congratulated Cogswell on the bank's performance. The board then gave him a round of applause. Dee Dee sat there glowing at this new recognition that Whit was receiving. She felt a great satisfaction that her hard work was finally paying off.

Chapter

85

Todd Christopher rushed into Dee Dee's office and announced, I have a plan for a new block of business that is an extension of the success in the mortgage sales we're experiencing. This is a killer idea!"

"Slow down, Todd. I'm in the middle of writing some reports and I'll be tied up all day. Come back about 5:30 and we can talk."

"Good, good. I'm meeting with a builder this afternoon. Is 6 o'clock OK?"

"I have so much to do that I'll be here even if you're late. See you then."

Christopher got back to the bank at 6:15. He was excited because he just sold a new builder who was looking for construction funding to build the infrastructure on a fifty-home parcel.

He pulled out a portfolio and began to take Dee Dee through the plan. He had statistics on all the mortgages they sold for both new homes and resales. He also had a chart on the age of each mortgage. His research showed at what point the average homeowner of a pre-owned home would be considering an upgrade or renovation. And because home values were increasing rapidly, there was a steadily growing amount of equity in these properties.

Todd recognized the opportunity to identify and sell this select group of mortgage customers a home equity line of credit. He called it a HELOC. It was a simple way for these homeowners to finance their renovations, which would further add to the already increasing value of their home. The HELOC principal would be protected by the equity. Based on their book of business, they could easily sell thousands of these loans.

After looking at his charts for some time, Dee Dee said, "I love your exuberance. This really is a great idea. Let's go have a drink and celebrate your new client, and this exciting concept for new business."

After a couple of Cosmos, Dee Dee began to come on to Todd, and he didn't resist. An hour later they were in her bed acting like rabbits on a mission.

When he left, Dee Dee said to herself, "I just recruited another soldier in my army." And as she thought about the evening she recognized that she was building a controlling relationship with all the top executives in the company. And she also admitted that the sex was becoming more and more fun, even if it was not fulfilling on an emotional level.

Chapter

86

At Whitney's suggestion, Dee Dee began to plan the bank's first customer appreciation dinner. She began by creating a budget and an approximate number of attendees. She then contacted her friend Kathy Cormier, who was a meeting and event planner.

A week later Kathy came into the office with her proposal that fell within the $25,000 budget. It included live music, a cocktail hour, and a three-course dinner for 150 people. Dee Dee had wanted a New York City location, but the cost jumped by nearly 40%. Instead, they decided on Nanina's in the Park, a beautiful venue located in Belleville.

Her next task was to put together an invitation list. Whitney had told her that he wanted to invite 30 people as his guests. When she added in the board members and their spouses, miscellaneous executives like herself, Shawn and some others, she was already at about 80 to 90 people. By allocating just one table of ten for each of the six ELT members who managed business centers, she was hitting her budget maximum.

Dee Dee had Shawn produce a simple but elegant invitation for distribution. She had one sent to each of the board members and the list of Whitney's friends. She gave four invitations to each of the gang of six, and sent the selected internal staff an invitation by email.

Within an hour the executives started showing up at her office.

Youngman was the first one in. He complained about only being able to invite four couples. He said, "How can I pick only four clients to invite? I manage hundreds of high net-worth clients and at least a score of them have accounts of $25 million each. I need at least three more tables."

That's out of the question, John. All of you are getting the same allocation. As it is, we're up to 150 people."

"There's only six of us who handle business sectors. With one table each, how did we get to 150?"

Well, there are the board members and other staff like me, for instance. And Whit has a large contingent of guests."

"Who could that asshole possibly be bringing to the event? He doesn't know any of our clients, except your family."

"Watch it John. He is working on several major clients that you don't know about. So drop it, and let me get back to work."

Each of the ELT members came to her office throughout the day with the same requests and questions. Both Mitchell and Christopher made a strong pitch to sit at Cogswell's table. All of the appeals, of course were denied.

On the night of the event, everyone was disappointed, but not surprised that Whit's table was insulated from the rest by being surrounded by his guest's and the board's tables. Whit's wife Lucille was seated on his left and Dee Dee on his right. Her guest was David Hacker, a board member and recent widower. All of the StarTrust executives were seething at how she set herself up to control the party. And they didn't miss noticing her familiarity with the board members, taking time to speak to each of them individually and meeting their spouses.

About halfway through the party, while Whit was visiting his friends at another table, Lucille slid into his seat and leaned over to Dee Dee and said in a soft voice, "I need to ask you a personal question." It was obvious that she had far too much to drink, but Dee Dee smiled and said, "Of course, Lucille. What would you like to know?"

"Are you sleeping with my husband?"

Shocked and shaken, she replied, "Lucille, that's absurd. Now you need to stop drinking and compose yourself. You are one of my dearest, lifelong friends. How could you even think that?" She then turned to David and said, "Lets take a walk to the bar."

As Dee Dee stood up, Lucille grabbed her arm and raised her voice loud enough for everyone at the table to hear and said, "Don't you dare blow me off. I know you're screwing him."

Pulling her arm away, she responded, "You're drunk. So please calm down and stop making these ridiculous accusations." And she and David walked off.

Hacker, who was a retired senior executive from Colgate, had been struggling for the last eight months with adjusting to his wife's passing. And while he was always a hard drinker, he had been fighting the temptation to let alcohol take over his life. He controlled his consumption at the banquet, but he was still quite tipsy by the end of the evening. When they were getting ready to leave, Dee Dee turned and said to him, "Dave, leave your car here, and I'll take you home. And tomorrow morning I'll arrange to have it brought to your house." Beginning to feel depressed, he was in no position to turn down the offer.

When they got to his house, Dee Dee came inside with him and said, "Let me help you get ready for bed." Before he could answer, she was removing his jacket. She brought him into the bedroom and with the lights out, took off the rest of his clothes and got him under the covers. She then took off her own dress and climbed in beside him. She began to tenderly hug him and kiss him. Within minutes he was fully aroused so she climbed on top of him and they fornicated to a surprisingly quick orgasm. Afterwards, he began to sob, and Dee Dee lay there for an hour holding him and gently rocking him to sleep. When he was completely under, she got dressed and left for home.

Chapter 87

There was a message marked urgent on Whitney's email account from Tiffany Hill to call as soon as possible. When Dee Dee responded for Whit, Tiffany explained her concern. "Hi Dee Dee, thank you for getting back to me. This is about the Luxury Auto Spa account. They make nightly deposits of cash, which is normal for a retailer, but lately we've noticed that the deposit amounts have increased substantially."

"Well, that shouldn't be an issue. They opened a second location. And they are probably doing very well. Whitney always boasts about their attention to detail and excellent customer service. He recommends them all the time."

"There's more to it than that. First of all, we get deposits at two branches every night, plus additional deposits during the day. And no deposit is ever more than $9,000. There have been days where their total deposit amount has surpassed $45,000. And the frequency of those large deposit days is increasing. To me, that's a red flag."

"And here's another one that's just as disconcerting. The company writes very few checks, which means they probably pay almost everything in cash. And finally, they make regular wire transfers to bank accounts in the Caribbean and in Mexico. Now, do I have your attention? By law, we have to report this. There are criminal penalties at risk here."

"Yes you have my attention. I will discuss this with Whitney right away. And thanks, Tiffany."

After she hung up, Dee Dee went right into Whit's office and told him about the odd banking activities. Whit wasn't concerned, and blew it off, saying, "If I reacted to every hysterical comment from the employees at this bank, I would never get any real work done. Just so you know, Pablo Alvarez told me that his business has been very successful and he has recently opened a few more locations. So that would account for the increase in deposit amounts. There is no reason for her to be alarmed, and certainly no need to notify the bank regulators. In fact, the last thing we want around here is to have bank examiners swarming all over our offices. Also, it is pretty normal for Hispanics from Mexico and elsewhere to be sending funds back home. And while it hurts our economy, there is not much we can do about it. So let the accounting department know what is going on, and to stay focused on all the important matters."

Dee Dee left his office satisfied with Whitney's explanation. She called Tiffany, who was not at all convinced by the response, but reluctantly gave in to Whit's justification. She said, "Well if Mr. Cogswell in not concerned, then I won't be either. But I have no choice but to fulfill my obligation and submit a report to him regarding these suspicions. Please urge him to take some action. Forwarding the report to the regulators would certainly fulfill his fiduciary responsibilities, even if it does prompt an audit."

Chapter  88

When Bobby Willis called Dee Dee to invite her to dinner, she had all to do to not laugh out loud. "So Bobby, I guess it's your turn at bat. When do you want to do this?"

"Are you free Wednesday? We could go to the Embassy Suites in Secaucus. They have a quiet bar that serves complimentary drinks and there's a casual restaurant where we can get something to eat."

"Well that will be a change of scenery, as I've never been there. I'll meet you there at seven."

When Dee Dee arrived, Willis was already at the bar, drinking a martini. Since the complimentary drinks were all well brands, she also ordered a martini. As the bartender prepared the drinks, she said, "Aren't the complimentary drinks for hotel guests? How do we qualify?"

"We qualify because I booked a room for the night."

"Isn't that a little presumptuous of you? Are you expecting me to sleep with you?"

"Dee Dee, I wasn't anticipating anything. All my expectations come in the form of surprises. And I get lots of them. But just so you know, I'm staying over because I have an appointment in Hackettstown in the early morning. So it's much easier to leave from here than from home."

As they drank their cocktails, Bobby made his pitch to either replace Cogswell or to become the Chief Operating Officer in order to accelerate the bank's growth. After he presented his plan and the rationale, Dee Dee said, "Look, I'll entertain any serious recommendations you have regarding the performance of the bank, but Whitney is staying exactly where he is. All of you need to understand that. If you think you can engineer a coup, then you're dreaming. You're all dreaming. So bring me your ideas, and I'll see about getting them pushed through. And I will also see that you get credit for them, so that down the road you can move up the ladder and not be on the same level as the others."

At that point they moved into the café and ordered dinner. He asked for a bottle of beer and she had a glass of wine. When dinner was over, Bobby asked Dee Dee if she ever tried cocaine. She was taken back by the question and quickly responded, "Of course not. I would never use anything like that. I mean, I've done pot a few times, and it's a pleasant high." And with a smile she added, "I also found that it heightens certain other responses. But I'm not interested in coke."

"Well, let me tell you about my new discovery. Recently, I found a new cocaine-like powder that is not addictive but delivers a much more intense euphoria than marijuana. Mitchell was introduced to it by Hector at the carwash. Let's go upstairs for a few minutes and you can try it. I promise it is amazing."

"Dee Dee was intrigued by Willis' description, so she went up to Bobby's suite and tried the new mystery substance. He took a snort and showed her how to do it. At first, she didn't feel any reaction, so she tried another hit. And then she got lost in this fast-paced, dreamy wonderland. She stood up, slipped off her shoes and began to unbutton her blouse. As Bobby stared at her, she announced, "I think we should have sex now." He took her from the sitting room to the bedroom and started taking off his clothes as she removed the rest of hers.

He looked at her full body and quickly became erect. She touched his penis and said, "Let's get under the covers." After exploring each other's bodies, Bobby climbed on top and inserted his member. They reached climax together and then rested a few minutes. Bobby then poured a couple of more lines and they each took another hit. From there they spent the next couple of hours enjoying each other, trying different positions.

At about 1 AM, Dee Dee got up, dressed and left for home. As she drove, she contemplated the strange turn of events that took place during the evening. She was still feeling the residual effects of the drug, which she really liked. She especially liked how it enhanced the sex. She never expected that Bobby would have booked a room at the hotel, or that he was into drugs. She also thought about the source of the drugs. She didn't make the connection at first, but now realized that the carwash actually was a money laundering front and a drug operation.

She also thought about how she was using the sexual activity to control the bank's executives. At this point she recognized that she could now more easily manipulate them, and she knew that they would do anything she asked. Dee Dee also reflected on her own reaction to the sex. She had not only become comfortable with the immorality of the activity, she was immensely enjoying it. But while she was looking forward to the next encounter, she recognized that it would never replace a true love relationship. And that was what she really craved.

After Dee Dee left the hotel, Willis was too wired to fall asleep, so he lay in bed reliving the sexual encounter with her. She certainly had a body built for sex and she knew how to use it. He also thought about her advice to him. Maybe he should make his move with her and work on becoming an EVP, moving ahead of the others. He decided to work on some recommendations on his own, and meet Dee Dee for dinner again to discuss his ideas. And maybe have another round of bed tennis.

Chapter 89

It seemed like StarTrust was really hitting stride. Every major division was expanding rapidly and the HR department was having trouble keeping up with the hiring of quality staff. Shawn DiPisa's marketing programs all delivered well beyond projections, and he was looking like a superstar. In an attempt to blunt the recognition and praise Shawn was receiving, all the other members of the ELT were personally taking the credit for each of their division's remarkable growth.

Bobby Willis boasted that the bank now had a record number of small business accounts, and as a result, much larger companies were starting to move their accounts to StarTrust.

The influx of business accounts heaped even more loans on Tom Mitchell's Commercial Loan Division. And Mitchell pointed out that it was his programs that had created an unprecedented demand for lending by a growing number of manufacturers, distributors and residential developers.

Hugo Sanchez had booked an enormous block of international loans that was delivering truly exceptional profits due to interest rates that were well above average.

Wealth Management and Trust Services, run by John Youngman was now doubling the fee income from previous years, with more and more high net worth families engaging the bank for wealth management and family trust services. With incomes rising across the board, even middle-income earners were becoming clients, looking for management of their investments.

All this activity contributed to Serena McCormack's Retail Branch Division, which just kept on adding locations.

But the biggest area of growth came from Todd Christopher's Home Mortgage Department. The housing market was like a runaway train, and StarTrust was getting mortgage applications from every corner of its multi-state service area. The biggest challenge was processing and closing the thousands of loan requests that were coming in, with no end in sight. In addition to the residential mortgages, the HELOC loan program was also growing well beyond expectations. While the home mortgages were sold off very quickly after closing, the HELOCs loans were serviced by the bank. So this book of business would deliver a long-term profit stream.

Dee Dee was preparing Whitney's presentation report for the year-end board meeting when she got a call from her uncle. Don suggested to her that all the members of the ELT attend this key meeting and each present their own report. "I want the executives to each be recognized for their own sector's contribution to the growth of StarTrust."

This directive caught Dee Dee by surprise. Quickly thinking she lied, "That's impossible Uncle Don. The entire Executive Leadership Team will be at a two-day offsite conference for a training and education session in Atlantic City on the evening of the board meeting. Whitney will be the only one in town. It's all booked and paid for. It's way too late to cancel it now."

"Well that's too bad. I should have called you sooner to get it set up. We'll look to schedule them for a meeting in the near future." After they hung up, she quickly made some calls including one to Kathy Cormier, the meeting planner she used for the appreciation dinner. She immediately scheduled the off-site for the days that coincided with the board meeting. And then she prepared an invitation under Whit's name for all to attend the mandatory session. The note mentioned some social activities including a golf outing so all the invitees were excited about the trip. She could have easily included herself in the offsite meeting and enjoy the perks of the two-day event, but she decided she would rather be at the board meeting, basking in the glory of Whit's success.

Of course, no one knew that the junket was actually replacing an opportunity for each of them to present their individual accomplishments in front of the board of directors. Shawn DiPisa, in particular would miss out on the chance to share the success generated by his remarkable communications programs. So, he would not get credit for the strategies and campaigns that were at the heart of the bank's incredible growth.

And poor Whitney was going to miss all the fun. He would have to sit through that dull meeting humbly accepting all the praise and credit for his valuable leadership. When all the event details were arranged, Dee Dee sat there elated by her decisive move. However, she may have felt differently if she knew Don's total agenda for the meeting.

On the night of the board meeting, when all the business reports were completed, Don announced a new stock distribution program. All the vice presidents, which included the six division VPs and Shawn DiPisa would each be awarded 100,000 shares of stock as a bonus for the incredibly successful year the bank had completed. Whitney Cogswell, as CEO would receive 150,000 shares. At $8.00 a share, this was an unbelievable windfall for all the executives. Over the previous three years, the team averaged about 10,000 shares a year. Middle managers usually received 500 to 1,000 shares, but this year they would receive 1,000 to 2,000 shares each.

Unfortunately, Dee Dee as a secretary, albeit an executive secretary, did not qualify for a stock bonus. She was very angry and disappointed that she did not participate in the distribution. But when she thought about it, she decided that she would talk to Whitney privately about a stock or cash bonus. He would find a way. After all, there was no way StarTrust would be enjoying this unprecedented success without her control over Whit and the entire executive staff. She realized that the board had no way of knowing her critical role in all this, but Whitney certainly did.

Part III

The Crash Heard Round the World

Chapter 90

The accolades were going to Whitney's head, and he began to believe that he personally was responsible for StarTrust's meteoric rise from a local bank chain to a regional powerhouse. Part of the misperception was that Dee Dee handled his tasks and decisions so deftly, that he had no idea what was involved in his role as CEO. In fact, he was convinced that all the entertaining he did at Ridgewood Country Club was the true source of their revenue. His cronies from college never missed an opportunity for a free round of golf or a tennis match that included lunch, dinner, or drinks. Occasionally, it would lead to some small piece of business that invariably resulted in no profit or worse, a high-maintenance business account or a loan that never got repaid.

So when Dee Dee came to him for a bonus, he was not very receptive. Instead he gave her a small salary increase, a car allowance and some additional perks. As an excuse, he cited the Board's decision to provide stock bonuses to executives only.

She was extremely disappointed in his meager response. While her goal was to make Whit very successful, what she wanted more than anything was his recognition of her contribution. Feeling unappreciated, she became depressed and began to once again make regular trips to the Italian bakery down the street.

But despite his mistreatment of her in this situation, she remained loyal, convinced that she could make him respect her role in the success he was perceived to accomplish. This lack of appreciation would not stand.

Chapter

91

Sanchez got an urgent call from the head of the Accounts Receivable Department. A lumber company in Paraguay had missed a payment. The wire transfer was due about a week ago and there was no response to the request for a payment date.

"Thanks for advising me of the situation. I'll check with the consultant and get back to you. If the funds arrive in the meantime, let me know."

Hugo called his contact at the consulting firm and they promised to follow up immediately. They explained that this particular mill harvested exotic woods used for architectural applications such as flooring, wall panels, and exposed wall and ceiling beams. They were also aware that demand had recently dropped due to a worldwide slowdown in the luxury residential housing market.

When Hugo got the call back, he was given nothing definitive in terms of the late payment. So he pressed further, "Look we need to know specifically when that payment will be wired. And we need to know now. If I am made aware of a problem, I could handle it easier. But they are stonewalling me, it is not going to help the situation."

"Mr. Sanchez, I apologize but I can't get to the decision maker. I will call you back as soon as I have a definitive answer."

Dissatisfied with the response, Hugo called the company directly, but was unable to speak to anyone with authority. Becoming concerned, he then phoned his loan department and instructed them to freeze the company's line of credit. Unfortunately, he was told they were at their limit and couldn't draw any more funds.

With that, he had no choice but to wait for the return call, that never came.

Chapter

92

It was Monday night, Whit's weekly card night. But this Monday, like many others, he wasn't playing cards. Once or twice a month, he had a clandestine rendezvous at Dee Dee's. On this evening, he showed up at her place and rang the doorbell. He heard her say, "It's open. Come on in." He entered the darkened apartment, turned and locked the door, and then tried to adjust his eyes. Whit could see her standing in the living room, her silhouette outlined in the ambient light coming from the window, so he walked towards her. As he got close, she said, "Stop there and take off your clothes, all of them." He complied, still trying to see what she was wearing. When she stepped closer to him, he could now make out the black corset, thong, mask and fishnet stockings she was wearing. As he turned to put his slacks on the couch, she struck his butt really hard with the flogger she was holding behind her back. "That's for the stock I didn't get."

"Holy shit that hurt. You broke my flesh. How am I going to explain that?"

"Easy. Just keep your tighty-whities on at home."
She then struck him again harder, saying, "And that's for the miserly raise you gave me."

Whitney was stunned by the severity of the blows, and stood there nervous about what was to happen next. In her other hand she had a device that she slid onto his limp penis and tightened it. When he looked down he realized that it was some kind of mini-leash that she used to walk him into the bedroom. She explained, "A couple years ago I attended this conference for single women. And all I heard was lonely women asking why they couldn't find a suitable partner. Finally, in frustration, I stood up and said, 'You women are pathetic. When are you going to take charge of your lives? Men are emotional cripples that have to be led around by the penis.' And with that, I got up and left. And now I have this little leash to fulfill that directive and lead you around by yours."

When she removed the leash, she ordered him to lay face down on the bed, and she proceeded to flog him some more, albeit with slightly less intensity. When he was ready to have an orgasm, she turned him over and tied his limbs to the bedposts. His penis stood erect, so she flicked it and the pain caused it to subside.

Dee Dee now stood over him, removed her thong and lowered herself onto his face. After her orgasm, she turned around, facing his feet, and lowered herself on his face again. She made him lick her until he was getting cramps in his jaw, all the while teasing his penis with strokes and licks. When she knew he was about to come, she turned around again and lowered herself on to his penis. He didn't last a minute before he exploded inside her. She managed to reach another orgasm before he became soft.

Dee Dee then got off the bed and went into the shower leaving Whitney still tied to the bed. Returning to the bedroom, she untied him and told him to get cleaned up and go home. She also demanded that he quickly find a way to adequately compensate her for his success. He simply nodded and mumbled, "I will take care of it."

Whit quickly showered, got dressed and left without saying another word. She lay there in bed smiling at how easy it was to control this pathetic excuse for a man.

Chapter

93

Todd Christopher placed a call to his largest builder client. Marden Homes had six housing developments in New Jersey and two in both New York and Pennsylvania. The company built over 400 homes a year in all price ranges.

"Charles, what's happening with business? We haven't seen a mortgage from any of your sites in two weeks. Is there a problem? Has another bank come in to try to undercut us?"

"Hi Todd. We're not sure what's happening. Homebuyers just stopped coming in to all our locations. We're sure it's not the mortgage rate increase, as most people aren't even aware that the rates went up. I will tell you we are getting concerned. In fact, I just ordered a flight of ads offering a package of free upgrades worth several thousand dollars. Hopefully that will kick start traffic again. I'll call you next week and let you know if we get any results. And I'll tell you. We'd better see some action. My entire operation is geared up to the sales volume that we've been booking over the last few years. I don't know how I would cut back without causing a lot of pain."

"OK, Charles. Definitely call me next week. In the meantime, I'm going to make some other calls. I'll let you know what I find out from a few of the other builders."

Christopher made calls to one of his smallest clients, as well as a couple that were mid size. And they all had the same report. Both traffic and sales were dropping precipitously. And no one had an answer. He then called a condo builder in Fort Lee and got a similar story. When he asked about the cause, the builder offered his opinion. "Todd. In my 20 years in business, I have never seen anything like this. We sell to a lot of real estate investors and speculators. I've got one guy that bought six units in my new building at pre-construction prices, and he will flip them before he has to close on them. But suddenly, I'm not seeing anybody coming into the showroom, not residential buyers or flippers. It's just dead. And if it stays like this, I'll be dead."

Now Todd was really concerned. He told all of the builders he had contacted to call him in a week with an update.

Chapter  94

Willis got a call one morning that he wasn't expecting at all. His block of small, entrepreneur business accounts had been increasing steadily, mostly because he kept the pressure on DiPisa to continue the advertising program that had been so successful.

Bobby had been basking in the glow of the big profits his sector was generating. So when he got a call from the Accounting Department, he was stunned. They explained that there were signs of trouble on a few fronts. Check overdrafts had suddenly surged from nearly none to several a day, all from the small business accounts. Nearly every company was maxing out their commercial lines of credit, and many were missing their payment dates on equipment loans. And making matters worse, a growing number of companies were closing their accounts, apparently going out of business.

Bobby asked, "Is this across the board, or are certain categories of business running into problems?"

"Good question. Best that we can tell is that it started out with mostly the construction-related companies, but now it is spreading out to other small businesses. The builders in particular that have construction loans with us are all falling behind on their payments."

"OK. I'll get my account staff to make some calls and see what's happening. In the meantime, keep me posted on any changes that occur."

Willis called in his account manager and instructed him to get a few people to start calling the accounts and find out what kind of problems they were encountering. And they were to report back to him ASAP.

The next morning Bobby's account Manager sent him an email confirming the downturn, but had no facts to point to its cause. He and his staff planned to go out into the field and meet directly with business owners and uncover any trends that were taking shape. Everyone was confident that it was a short-term phenomenon. But was that just wishful thinking?

Chapter 95

At the following ELT meeting, Willis shared the findings of his staff with the other members in the room. Small Business appeared to be on the front edge of a downturn that had its beginnings in the home building field. Many companies that were sub-contractors or provided services to the homebuilders were rapidly falling victim to the unexplained slowdown. But the contagion was now quickly spreading to all types of businesses, both large and small.

Todd Christopher spoke up and confirmed that the home construction sector was experiencing a slowdown, and this could be playing a role in the downturn. He deliberately soft-pedaled the rapid pace the dramatic decline was taking, where homebuilders were going from waiting lists of buyers to no buyers on the horizon. He had hopes that this setback would be a short-lived blip in overall sales growth. And everyone else in the meeting had the same optimism.

Cogswell, who took the unusual step to attend this particular meeting, downplayed the entire reports from both ELT members. He said, "The economy is on fire. Our challenge is keeping up with all the business, not worrying about a brief interruption in activity. I am planning to further increase our marketing efforts, and add more staff as needed. And although it has not been announced yet, we may be acquiring another bank. But that is still under wraps and at this time is still confidential."

Serena spoke up first. "Whit, what bank are you negotiating with?"

"I cannot say yet. We are not even close to the signing and I do not want to get into a discussion and spook it."

Mitchell jumped into the fray and advised, "There are several early signs of weakness and we'd be wise to tread softly until we know for sure if the economy is faltering." The other members began to pile onto Tom's statement, supporting his position.

Dee Dee, seeing that Whit was losing control of the meeting, ended it with her remark, "Whitney has been looking at data and he is in a very good position to determine the status of the business marketplace. Before we take any drastic steps, we'll be certain we are on solid ground. So let's call the meeting, unless anyone else has some new business."

When the meeting ended, Dee Dee followed Whit into his office and asked, "What bank are you looking to acquire?"

"Oh I mentioned it to you recently. At the banquet, I reconnected with one of my classmates who heads up a bank in New Haven called Central Connecticut Bank & Trust. They have been buying up small, single-branch banks all over the state and are now struggling with overheated growth. We have the infrastructure and can buy them at below market value."

"Have you told the board about this?"

"Not yet. I just signed the letter of intent. If they sign it, I'll bring it to the board for their blessing."

"Whitney, that's not how it works. You don't have the authority to sign an acquisition letter. What if the board rejects it? That bank can then sue us if the deal falls through. And worse, they can sue you personally. You'd better talk to Don Davino right away."

"OK, OK. I will give him a call before the end of the day. It is not like I am concluding a deal here. I am just moving the process to the point where the lawyers and accountants can take over."

"Well if you signed anything on behalf of the bank, I hope you ran it by Linda Honeycheck."

"I did not get to do that, but I can read a legal document. After all I did take many law courses in college."

About an hour later, Whit got a call on his cell from Franklin Blauvelt, the CEO of the New Haven bank. "Whitney, you old dog. I was planning to drive to New Jersey later today. I will be staying at the Park Ridge Marriott. If you are available for dinner, I will bring the non-disclosure and some of the other paperwork, so we can move this deal forward."

"That sounds great. I will meet you at the bar there at 5:30. We can have dinner at the hotel's restaurant, and get the documents signed."

"I will see you there. And why don't you book us some late night *entertainment* for after dinner."

"That I can do. I will see you later."

When Cogswell got to the bar, his fraternity brother was already there, enjoying his martini. They shook hands, exchanged pleasantries, and began going over the paperwork. Both executives were anxious to get through the business portion of their meeting so they could enjoy the evening. Whitney signed the non-disclosure, and looked over the base terms of the deal. Franklin advised, "By counter signing the term sheet, you agree to the key points of the contract that we shook on last week. Once that is done, the lawyers can complete the due diligence and hammer out the details."

Confirming that everything was in order, Whit signed the document. Once completed, Blauvelt noted, "I'm impressed that you could move so fast on this deal. I was concerned because, as I explained, there is another bank that has been pitching us, and I found out Friday that they are preparing to sweeten the offer that we rejected. It's gratifying that you recognized our value and were willing to meet our asking share price."

"Franklin, It's a good deal, not a great deal. But StarTrust will benefit from the acquisition, and you will walk away with a lucrative exit package. I still have to get board approval, but that's a formality at this point. They will follow my lead."

With the paperwork out of the way, they moved into the dining room, had dinner and then returned to the bar. Waiting there were two attractive women that Whitney had arranged for them to meet. They went up to Blauvelt's suite where Franklin had a couple of bottles of champagne on ice. With jackets and ties removed, they began to drink the bubbly, celebrating the deal. When they opened the second bottle, more clothes came off and the real party began. One of the girls turned off the lights, and with just the night light in the room, they then began performing various combinations of twosomes, threesomes and everybody in the sandbox.

Sometime after midnight, Whit departed the hotel with the euphoria of the evening leaving him feeling overly proud of himself. Here he was negotiating bank acquisitions as part of his role as the CEO of one of the largest regional financial institutions in the northeast. And the perks that he was able to provide to himself and his college friend just added to his sense of power.

Everyone made it sound so difficult to succeed in business, starting with Shawn when he took over the marketing. But almost immediately, he hit stride, and if Don hadn't prematurely killed his radio campaign, it would have been the most successful promotion in the chain's history. And now his leadership at the bank, where everyone was certain he would fail, was delivering a series of unprecedented successes. Whit thought that it wouldn't be a stretch if he were recruited for CEO by some national bank in the very near future.

Chapter

96

Dee Dee had an appointment with her doctor, as she was having problems dealing with all the stress of the job. She complained that the anti-depressants were contributing to her weight gain, but yet she wanted a stronger dose. "Doctor, is there a different brand I can try that would help my anxiety, but have less effect on my weight?"

"Miss Davino, we can try a stronger dose of a different brand but there's very little chance it will impact your weight control. It's important that you maintain the diet regimen I provided you and do more exercise. Get a personal trainer who can help you with a workout program that can facilitate the reduction of some of the pounds you've gained.

"You need to make this a priority. Combining stress, depression and excessive weight is the worst possible recipe for good health. I can't emphasize strongly enough that you have to take positive steps now."

She left the doctor's office with the prescription, went to the pharmacy and had it filled. As she left the store, she popped two pills immediately thinking this would help her relax. Of course, the prescription did help, but it took a few days for her to actually feel its effect.

She had been struggling with the challenges that Whit created for her. Lately it was getting so difficult dealing with him, plus all the added pressure from the ELT members.

After visiting the fitness center and renewing her exercise regimen, she began to feel better about herself. She then went to the office with renewed energy, better enabling her to handle all the problems she faced. Her first stop when she arrived at the bank was to go to Human Resources. In a private meeting with Eric Dawson, the VP who ran the department, she sought out his advice about the sexual harassment issues she was facing in the executive suite. While she didn't want to file a formal complaint, she did want to go on record that she was a victim. In addition to the document that was placed in her personnel file, she volunteered to approach the offender in an effort to defuse the situation.

Chapter

97

While Dee Dee was at the doctor's office, Whit got a call from the commercial loan department. Endless Energy was late on a balloon payment for $400,000. Whitney was shocked and said, "Who is Endless Energy? And why is it me you are calling about this?"

The loan clerk said, "I'm calling you because you are the officer that originated the loan for $2 million. And right now I'm concerned about the entire balance."

It then struck Whit who the company was. He said, "I will make a call and get back to you."

He then placed a call to his college buddy Reginald Nimmy to find out why the payment date was missed. When Nimmy called back he explained, "Unfortunately, the government cancelled the contract. The patented product worked perfectly in the lab, but the company could not produce the energy in bulk. The DOD therefore walked away from the deal."

"So how the hell do we get our loan paid? This is a serious amount of money."

"Come on Whit, this is small change for a bank like yours. You have a lien on the patent rights, so take it over and sell it to an energy developer. You'll probably double your money."

When he hung up, a furious Cogswell called Linda Honeycheck and told her about the call from Nimmy. She was aghast. And after asking several background questions about the deal, she said, "Whit, I never saw this loan application. Where is the lien document that serves as collateral for this loan? The file you sent me showed the patent approval, but how did you determine that the value of the patent is worth $5 million? Get all the documentation and paperwork sent to my office immediately. This entire transaction reeks of fraud. And once again your incredible failure of judgment is nothing short of inexcusable."

Chapter 98

It was Monday morning when teams of FBI agents showed up at the three bank branches where Luxury Auto Spa made their deposits and immediately shut them down. At the same time, they raided the four car wash locations, arresting all employees, and confiscated all computers, file cabinets storage cases and anything related to managing the business. At each facility they also found large quantities of prescription drugs and various controlled substances, plus several guns and storage boxes full of cash. The third prong of the foray was StarTrust headquarters. One team went right to the IT center and immediately put a halt to all outbound wire transactions. Another team went to the retail branch on the ground floor and halted all transactions. The largest team, headed by the agent in charge, went up to the executive offices and ordered all the ELT members into the conference room.

A very indignant Whitney came out of his office and began shouting at the agents, before Dee Dee could stop him. She grabbed both his arms and said, "Do you want to get arrested? Get into the conference room and follow their exact instructions. And tell everyone not to say a word until our attorney shows up. And you do the same. I will call Linda Honeycheck and tell her to get right up here."

All the executives came into the room visibly shaken by the presence of this many armed FBI investigators. When everyone was assembled and seated, the lead agent turned his attention to Whit. "Mr. Cogswell, I'm Agent William Meddis. We're here because of the bank's ongoing money laundering scheme with known drug dealer Jose Alvarez."

Despite Dee Dee's admonition to remain silent, Whitney burst out, "That is outrageous! Ultimate Car Wash is a legitimate local business that deals in large volumes of cash. You can be sure there is absolutely no money laundering taking place at our bank."

At the same time Dee Dee came into the room and glared at Whitney and announced, "Linda Honeycheck, our corporate attorney will be here in ten minutes. In the meantime, no one will answer any questions until she arrives."

The announcement calmed some of the ELT members, but others remained wary.

Meddis turned to Whit. "Have it your way. We have shut down your entire IT processing facility, so no funds can come in or go out unless or until we approve the resumption of activity. And that could take all day. StarTrust BanCorp is facing fines of up to several hundred thousand dollars, and some of you could be charged criminally. So the sooner we get some cooperation, the easier it will be for all parties. I hope you realize that we could shut down the bank permanently over this extraordinary protracted breach."

With that last comment, John Youngman jumped up and shouted at Meddis, "You can't shut us down. We're too big to fail."

At the same time Whitney began to respond to the agent, but Dee Dee kicked him visibly under the table to stop him. And simultaneously she said to Youngman, "John, shut up now. We have orders to await our attorney."

A few minutes later Honeycheck rushed into the room, looked around and addressed the lead agent. "I'm Linda Honeycheck, corporate attorney for StarTrust. You have a search warrant I trust? Can I see it? And what are the charges you're claiming against our institution?"

Agent Meddis produced a large sheaf of papers and handed it to her. The search warrant was properly signed and seemed to be in order, but she was surprised at some of the charges. Money laundering had become a catchall with all the drug enforcement activity around the country. And she knew that banks could easily become ensnarled in the technicalities of transferring cash. This she chalked up to sloppy processing and reporting. But what got her attention was deliberate complicity by the bank in the effort, plus the charges that some executive employees were customers of the drug dealer. These were unexpected revelations that shaped up as a strong case against the bank.

She looked up and asked Meddis, "Agent Meddis, on what grounds are you claiming that the bank knowingly aided and abetted this alleged conspiracy to launder money? That's a very strong charge."

"Ms. Honeycheck, if you take the time to go through the entire file, you will see documents that support the charges. There is a record of phone calls as well as a memo from the IT staff to Mr. Cogswell and other staff reporting suspicious activity on this account and classic movement of illicit funds. There are also affidavits from our undercover field agents, along with photos of your executives making drug purchases from employees at the car wash. This includes not just Mr. Cogswell, but others that are sitting around this table. We've actually had an agent working undercover there for the last several months."

With that bombshell announcement, everyone was in near panic. Whitney was apoplectic at being exposed like a criminal on such a minor activity as buying a bag of marijuana. Linda remained calm and asked the agent, "Can I make a request that you allow everyone to return to their desks, so you and I can privately go over the evidence and get this issue resolved?"

Meddis responded, "Yes Ms. Honeycheck, we can do that. OK, everyone. Return to your desks, but no phone calls, not even on your cells. My agents will be monitoring you."

With the room cleared, Honeycheck could now talk freely. "All right Meddis, what do you want? What will it take to make this go away quietly?"

"We can make it go away, but it will be very expensive and it won't be quiet. We need to make examples of the car wash, and the bank. This was such a blatant breach that I can't just have you pay a fine."

"Let's start with the money. How much are we talking about?"

"This is a large six figure lapse of fiduciary duty. I can't see it being less."

"I think that's too high, but we'll talk about that in a minute. How about we take this position. The FBI, while investigating a local drug dealer, uncovered a complex money-laundering scheme that involved StarTrust BankCorp. When made aware that their bank was being used to funnel money, the bank's management cooperated with the FBI to trace the movement of the funds, recover a large amount of money, and bring the dealer to justice. We can spin this into a story that makes the FBI look really good without tarnishing the bank's reputation."

"The concept is somewhat agreeable, but there are a lot of loose ends. First, we control the story with the press. Second, the fine is $500,000. Next, you claw back an additional $250,000 from the funds that just have been transferred through ACH/electronic debit during the last 24 hours, and any other resource that is holding these illicit funds, all of which we will then confiscate. And fourth, you fire four of your executives including the CEO, who have been regular customers of Alvarez, for complicity in abetting the money transfers. But before we conclude the terms of the deal, I will have to get confirmation from the Director."

"We are not firing the CEO, and that is not negotiable. He is highly regarded by the board and if you cite him, it makes the whole escapade that much worse and harder to justify the terms of the deal. The board will not approve the deal and then we'll have to go into litigation. And none of us want that. And besides, he was just a pot smoker. The rest of the terms sound fair. I will want our communications officer, Shawn DiPisa to approve the text of the announcement before you make it. And there's a chance that we can claw back some of the transferred funds if they went out in the last 24 hours. If we're able to deliver more than the 250K, we want the fine reduced by that same amount.

Now, who are the other three execs?"

"Thomas Mitchell, John Youngman and Robert Willis have become heavy cocaine users, so you don't want them on your staff anyway. And we can use them as scapegoats in enabling the scheme. Cogswell as you pointed out was a weed smoker, so it's a little easier to overlook his bad judgment. But with that concession, we'll want to raise the fine to $750,000. In addition, he will have to testify against Alvarez."

Relieved that Whitney's job would be saved, Honeycheck agreed to the settlement. She knew he would never allow anything that damaged his personal reputation. She was also aware that he was the real culprit. This disaster, like the others had his fingerprints all over it.

When Linda went into Whit's office to explain the terms to him, he was a nervous wreck. Having little patience for his shortcomings, she said, "Look Whit. I just saved your ass. Again. You're getting away with a reasonable fine and there will be no personal charges against you, but you have to testify against Pablo Alvarez."

"I can't do that. He's such a nice guy. He's a family man supporting all those immigrants and their families. Besides, where am I going to go to get my Vette detailed?"

"Will you listen to yourself, you sniveling little shit. He's a drug dealer. People's lives have been destroyed because of him. Three of your key executives are being fired. And trust me, he doesn't support immigrants. He preys on them, just like he preys on assholes like you. So you're going to sign this agreement with the FBI. You're going to testify against Alvarez, and you're going to have to move quickly to get the IT department to see how much of his money we can salvage and recover. Right now, I'm going down to HR and take care of the terminations."

Chapter  99

None of the ELT staff left their offices the rest of the day, and no one made any outgoing calls. They just sat at their desks stunned, and waiting to see what land mine would explode next.

About an hour after the FBI left the premises, The VP of Human Resources, Eric Dawson came up to the executive suite with six of his staff. He went into Whit's office, while the others split into teams of two and went to offices of Willis, Mitchell, and Youngman. He explained to Cogswell what was about to transpire with the three executives and had him sign the termination orders. At the same time each team presented their respective officer with his termination agreement, detailing the terms, and had them sign it. The agreement called for a six-month severance package, an immediate loss of all their benefits, but they were able to retain their shares of StarTrust stock and their 401Ks. The HR team members then stood by while they each packed their personal belongings and turned in their cell phones, laptops, keys and ID tags. Dawson went into each office and asked if there were any questions. He then escorted them down to their cars and watched them leave the garage.

Serena sat in her office watching the drama while she held back tears. She realized that this entire episode could have been avoided. Had Whitney shut down the bank accounts of the car wash, there would have been no repercussions for the drug use by her three colleagues. And at worst, the bank would have gotten away with a slap on the wrist and a small fine. She realized that now more than ever, she had to get closer to Dee Dee. If she could only gain her confidence, she could influence the advice she gave Whit. This could be an opportune time. Dee Dee's failure to control Whit's decision on the car wash issue would give Serena an opening to become her confidant. Could this tragedy finally be the opportunity to turn her?

Sanchez and Christopher, seeing how swiftly the scene played out, each realized just how vulnerable they were. They, like the others had always felt that Cogswell's weaknesses were a benefit to their job security at the bank. This conclusively proved otherwise.

After her visit to the HR department, Linda Honeycheck went to DiPisa's office and explained the next steps to him. The FBI would prepare and forward the text of their announcement to be read at the yet unscheduled press conference. Shawn was to review the copy and make only necessary edits. He was then to write the bank's statement that he would read at the news event. She advised him that she would make the final approval of both drafts, and that he should be prepared to respond to questions from the press. Linda advised him that she would forward a brief that contained possible questions with appropriate answers to get him ready for the conference.

Shawn felt that he could put a positive spin on this potentially disastrous development, and he called Laura to explain what was happening. She suggested they prepare a few advertorials and follow up press releases to bring public opinion back in favor of the bank. She also suggested that StarTrust make a substantial donation to a drug rehab facility with some press fanfare.

Dee Dee sat at her desk seething at how she had failed Whit. This was one disaster that she could not contain. And yet it could have been far worse. Linda Honeycheck did an excellent job of protecting him, and salvaging the bank's image.

She called her uncle and filled him in on the massacre that took place in the executive suite that day. Don sat there listening to her detailed explanation and hung his head. "We will get past this challenge, Dee Dee. Don't take it personally. I will call an emergency board meeting and we will plan our next steps."

Chapter

100

When everyone had left at the end of this somber day, Serena walked down to Dee Dee's office and sat down at her desk. Dee Dee looked up but did not turn around. "Serena, this is not a good time. I'm really busy straightening out this mess. What do you need?"

"Dee Dee, I realize this isn't the time, but I need to talk to you. If I were more aware of what is going on, I could help you better manage Whit. This disaster today could have been prevented. Can we get together after work one day soon? If I had had your trust and confidence, together we may have been able to eliminate this issue before all this damage occurred."

Before she could answer, her phone began to ring. Ignoring it she responded, "Look Serena, I haven't heard from you in weeks. I'm not even sure how you feel about me anymore. I've got calls coming in on two lines, so please send me an email with some dates, and we'll get it set up."

The next morning Serena sent Dee Dee an email with a few dates over the next two weeks. Responding to Dee Dee's comment, she added a footnote apologizing for not seeing her in a few weeks, and confirming that her goal as stated previously was for their close personal friendship to grow into a lasting intimate relationship.

A few days later, Serena still hadn't heard back from Dee Dee. So feeling dejected, she pondered what her next step should be. Laura had just come into the bank to meet with Shawn and go over the public relations plan she developed. When she saw Serena, she stopped by her office and sat down. A second cousin of Laura's had married Serena a few years back and after a brief period it ended in a messy divorce. The two women had remained friends and saw each other occasionally after the bank reorganization. Serena always found Laura to be an attentive listener and concerned advocate. So she was grateful for this encounter.

Laura noticed her depressed demeanor and asked, "Is that money laundering disaster still bothering you? You look terrible."

"You're right. I'm in a funk and this black Monday is only part of it. "I'm not sure if Shawn shared all the details with you, but the entire issue, including the firings could have been easily avoided." She went on to explain how she was working on getting close to Dee Dee to help her manage Whitney's weaknesses. More recently however, she had begun to reject Serena's offers to help. Had Dee Dee only shared the problem with the car wash monies, Serena would have pushed her to stop the transactions. Serena deliberately left out her romantic involvement with Dee Dee as she wasn't sure how much of that to share with Laura. She then explained that right after the raid, Serena again approached Dee Dee to work together to prevent the next fiasco. But she didn't get a response, and now she feels rejected.

"Serena, it is common knowledge that Whit is not up to the task of running a bank this size, or any size for that matter, particularly on his own. And with the kinds of challenges StarTrust is encountering, Dee Dee is also out of her league. She needs support and you are probably the best one to provide it. If you don't mind, I'm going to share our conversation with Shawn. He and Dee Dee are pretty close. Maybe he can intercede."

"Oh thank you Laura. That would be wonderful. I really want to get close to Dee Dee again."

As Laura left to go down to Shawn's office her antenna went up.

She had just observed that Serena's mood changed entirely with her last sentence. It made her wonder what that was all about.

After she and Shawn concluded their work on the program, she shared her conversation with Serena, and asked him to speak to Dee Dee. He fully agreed that something had to be done. The bank could not handle another hit like this last one.

Chapter 101

As Whit sat smoldering in his office, the call came in from Blauvelt. "Whitney my brother. How goes it this great morning? Have you completed your due diligence so we can conclude our deal? My time is getting short as I have to move my wife to a cancer treatment center in California."

"Franklin, StarTrust is going to have to delay this acquisition. We ran into an unexpected issue with the bank regulators. In an effort to justify their existence, they brought in the FBI on some money transfer technicality and we are going to be fined and possibly sanctioned." Cogswell deliberately left out the pertinent details of the damning actions that led to the raid. He also knew that there was no possibility that the bank would approve his recommendation to acquire a bank at this time.

Blauvelt was stunned. He desperately needed to complete this deal before his bank failed. Feeling the pressure, he coaxed Whit, "Oh come now. That kind of activity by the regulators happens all the time. I am sure the fine will be modest, particularly for a bank your size. So use your position as CEO and get our deal on a fast track. I know you want it as much as I do."

"I am truly sorry Franklin, but we are not going forward with this acquisition at this time. I have too much to deal with to be putting time in on a purchase of a bank this small."

Near panic, Blauvelt now threatened him, "Now you listen to me carefully Cogswell. You signed a contract to purchase our bank and I will enforce that contract. I will give you 24 hours to respond in the affirmative, or we will file suit and notify the banking commission. If you are in trouble with the regulators now, this action may push you off a cliff. And I would hate for word to get out that you came to my hotel room with two prostitutes in an effort to get me to sell our bank to you."

At about the same time Whitney was pounding his fist on the desk in response to Blauvelt's phone call, Hugo Sanchez walked into Dee Dee's office. His roving eyes immediately noticed that her breasts seemed even larger than when he was last with her. But he also picked up on the fact that the rest of her body was also expanding exponentially. And he thought distractedly, "What a waste of beautiful tits on that overweight body."

"Hugo, why are you standing there looking me over? Is there something I can do for you?"

"I was admiring your full figure," he lied. "When can I see you again?"

"Look I'm way too busy for this bullshit. Now get out of here."

"Dee Dee, I did come over to discuss some serious business with you, but you get me so aroused, I want to take you right here in the office. But please accept that as a compliment."

Smiling she asked, "So what business issue do you want to discuss?"

"Have you been seeing all the delinquency reports this week? We're facing a major crisis with our offshore clients. They are all in default and I'm actually having trouble contacting some of them. Most of my clients are commodity producers, lumber companies, miners, and such. And with the slowdown in the housing sector, there's no market for their products. We could be facing massive losses in our loan portfolio, and I wanted to bring it to Whitney's attention. We are going to have to take legal action to protect our interests. Linda Honeycheck needs to be made aware of the situation, as I'm sure we will need international legal representation. I think we should talk about it at the next ELT meeting."

"Yes, I saw the reports and I'm aware of the situation. It's on my agenda to discuss with Whitney."

"OK, good. I'm just trying to go on record and avoid any surprises like last week. So when can we hook up?"

Before she could respond to his invitation, Todd Christopher came up and stuck his head in her office. She turned to him and said, "Hugo was just leaving. Is there something I can help you with Todd?"

Todd sat down and set a stack of reports on her desk. "I just got the latest delinquency reports and they are much worse than expected. We have major issues all across the board. I've cut off funding for several of our builder clients, and I'm trying to stop the bleeding at some of others. But I'm afraid our loan portfolio is going to be hammered."

"Yes Todd, I know. I've got copies of those reports already. And I plan to talk to Whitney about them."

With that, her phone rang and she answered it as she motioned Christopher to leave. "This is Dee Dee. How can I help you? Oh, Hi Uncle Don, how are you?"

"I'm not well at all dear. Suddenly the car wash catastrophe over the money laundering seems like a small problem. Now we are having issues with Two Wyse Guys and that in turn is causing problems with Donny's operation. I set Monday evening as the date for the unscheduled board meeting, and I want everyone on the ELT to be at that meeting. Make sure they are all there. No junkets, no excuses."

Chapter  102

Later that day Shawn walked into Dee Dee's office and saw the stress on her face. He could see that she was on the verge of tears. She looked up and transformed into a radiant smile, saying, "Finally a friendly face. Shawn you have no idea of the kind of day I've been having. In addition to some disastrous bank problems, I'm having issues with my medication. I don't like to talk about this, but I'm so comfortable with you. I've been on anti-depressants for a long time now, which as you can see makes it difficult for me to control my weight. Lately the meds haven't been as effective, so the doctor switched to a stronger prescription. The new formula doesn't agree with me so I stopped taking them and I'm trying to tough it out." And as she was telling him this, she began to well up.

"Dee Dee, you are taking on way too much, and I understand why. But you can't do it all yourself. I came to talk to you about this very issue.

"When it comes to difficult banking situations, instead of facing them alone, I'm urging you to seek advice from Serena. She can really help you navigate the system. She has lots of experience and she wants to help."

With the mention of Serena's name, Dee Dee went into a rage, her face contorted and turned red. "Shawn, I can't believe you're betraying me like this. That woman is a witch. All she wants to do is get Whitney fired, so she can become the CEO. She doesn't want to help me. She wants to destroy me. You don't know what she's done to me and how she has hurt me. You'd be shocked."

Shawn immediately recognized the irrational behavior that was taking place in front of him, and he realized that he was not equipped to deal with it. "Dee Dee, I'm sorry I upset you but you need to get back on some kind of medication right away. We can talk more when you are in a calmer state. Again, I'm sorry for adding to your distress."

Shawn was very troubled watching Dee Dee break down, as he had never seen a reaction like that from a woman he was conversing with. He called Laura and told her what happened. Laura became upset and told him that she was also concerned for Dee Dee. She suggested that he let her calm down, and go back to her office in a little while and suggest she take the rest of the day off.

As soon as Shawn left her office, Dee Dee removed a document from a folder and marched down to HR. She handed Dawson the sheet of paper, which contained a printout of a recent email that she received from Serena McCormack and announced, "I tried to reason with her, but she keeps trying to push me into a relationship. I can no longer work with her or be in her company. I've been having nightmares over this and I'm now ready to sign a formal complaint to have her removed from the company. Look at me. I am so distraught that I can't continue to work today. I'm going home to rest and regain my composure."

Dee Dee left the building knowing that the expected termination would take place while she was at home. There was no way she could face Serena or witness her removal from the office under those circumstances.

As it turns out, the bank had a process for dealing with these issues. Dawson called Serena and asked her to come to his office as soon as possible. She came right down expecting an issue with one of her branch staff. So she was shocked when he blindsided her with Dee Dee's complaint. After a heated discussion that included her very strenuous denials, she became further frustrated. Dawson told her that she was to have no contact with Dee Dee, except in the presence of other staff. And as of now, he was putting her on notice. Serena stood up and said, "Like hell you are. You will have my resignation letter by day's end. And if I don't get my full severance package, you can expect a really ugly lawsuit."

Chapter 103

The uniformed Federal Marshal surprised Whit by walking into his office unannounced, handed him a large envelope, and asked him to sign the receipt. His timing was impeccable as he arrived shortly after Dee Dee had taken the rest of the day off.

Having no idea what the envelope contained, Whitney tore it open and read the first page. As he read the complaint filed by Blauvelt and his bank, he went into an angry outburst, tearing the pages of the documents and throwing them into his trash bin.

When he had calmed down, he put in a call to Franklin to tell him of the absurdity of this lawsuit. However, he was unable to reach him, so he left a blistering message, threatening to crush him and his insignificant bank. Feeling better about the thought that his strong message would convince Blauvelt to back off, Whit left the office and decided to take a joyride in his Corvette. Riding at high speed in the sleek sports car was therapy for him, as it always calmed him down.

He was doing 95 mph on the New Jersey Turnpike when the trooper pulled him over. The officer explained that his excessive speed in a construction zone would result in a double penalty for speeding of more than $400 plus five points on his license, and a 30-day suspension. In addition, he would be required to appear in court. Without saying anything to the trooper, Whit tore up the ticket and tossed the pieces on the passenger seat. As the trooper turned around to return to his squad car, Whit left the scene by burning rubber for 100 yards, fishtailing back onto the highway. As he drove off, the traffic ticket fragments began to blow out onto the road. The trooper jumped in his car, chased down Whit and pulled him over a second time. He then wrote two more tickets, one for littering and one for careless driving. As he handed the tickets to Whit, he said, "My name is Officer George Cranmer. I am not supposed to lecture you when I write you a summons. But you can be sure that I will be in the courtroom on your appearance date. Do not expect any mercy or plea-bargaining from the court, even if you bring a lawyer to represent you. And if you don't show up, a warrant will be issued for your arrest.

"Oh, and by the way, here's a little tip for you. Adding what you think is that clever quote *Blew By You* on the rear deck of your Vette only serves to really piss people off. Have a good day, sir."

Whit got off the highway and started driving aimlessly along the quieter back roads in the southern part of the state. Unfortunately, the encounter with the trooper conflicted with his expected therapy.

Chapter 104

The board meeting started exactly on time, despite the fact that not everyone had arrived. Missing were two board members and Cogswell. Don Davino began the meeting by introducing a guest, Economist Raymond Stern.

The consultant stood and began a PowerPoint presentation on the current state of the economy. His assessment was dire. The residential housing market had expanded to the point that a bubble had formed. And if it weren't controlled very quickly it would burst, bringing all residential construction rapidly to a halt. It was poised to be the perfect storm for financial destruction. The federal government had been and continued to encourage consumers to purchase homes using Fannie Mae and Freddie Mac to fund the mortgages. Credit was so loose that anyone who can sign their name was deemed to be eligible to purchase a home. In an effort to keep up with demand, the entire home building channel was overextended with purchases of land, construction material, equipment, staff, inventory, etc. And because of the escalation in home prices, values were overinflated. This allowed homeowners to take out home equity lines of credit, further exacerbating the financial stability of the entire country. And the zooming prices were attracting an inordinate amount of mostly unqualified speculators and flippers to the housing market, increasing the frenzy and further driving up the numbers.

As Stern completed the presentation, there was silence from the stunned group. Everyone knew there were problems, but no one realized the extent of the looming crisis. Finally, one of the board members who came in just after the presentation began, asked, "How long do you think this slowdown will last?"

Stern replied, "We're hoping it's a short term phenomenon. There is still plenty of confidence in the market and in the economy as a whole. We expect to see a turnaround begin within the next few months. However, with homebuilding stalled, it will take a while for it to regain momentum. And I don't expect it to return to the heady days we've recently experienced. There is no liquidity in the market, so you can expect a fair amount of pain. This will occur as we adjust to resuming activity, and at the same time begin scaling back from full production. You can also expect layoffs across the board, even in industries not related to housing. And there will certainly be a sharp deflationary trend in home prices. When this occurs, it will cause a lot of homeowners to be underwater with their mortgages, and in particular those who also have HELOCs. I hope the importance of that fact is not lost on you."

The same gentleman then asked, "Can you explain why that would be critical if people continue to make their mortgage payments?"

If the scenario plays out according to all that the data indicates we will fall into a truly deep recession, and possibly a depression. We just don't know what the economy can handle. If either of those results ensues, then people will have trouble paying their mortgages. And if they can't make their mortgage payments, then you will be dealing with foreclosures and short sales in unimaginable numbers."

Don spoke next, "Mr. Stern, what happens if we don't get the expected bounce back? What is the worst case scenario?"

"Investors and speculators drove the market to its heights, and they are the ones that are now dropping out at the first sign of slowdown. If they don't move back into the market, you will see the worst bloodbath since the Great Depression. Now before you panic, keep in mind that the Fed and other government agencies are watching the situation and will intercede if the situation gets any worse.

"Mr. Davino, despite the safeguards that are in place, plus the likelihood of a return to normalcy, my advice is to reduce your exposure and your overhead, and prepare to hunker down for the long haul."

"Thank you Mr. Stern. If there are no more questions, I will ask you to leave so we can digest what we learned and continue our board meeting. You have been most enlightening."

As Stern left, Don turned to Sid Wyse and said, "Mr. Wyse, as a board member and one of the largest bank customers, I had asked you to make a report on the financial health of Two Wyse Guys appliance chain. Are you prepared to make that report?"

"Thank you Mr. Davino. Our store chain is the largest independent retailer in the northeast. And in addition to retail, we have built a very large wholesale appliance business that caters to small to mid-size homebuilders. Our sales at this unit have suddenly dropped substantially in both categories and we have three warehouses full of inventory.

With all the HELOC money that was on the street, everyone was renovating their homes. Simultaneously, the contractors were building houses as fast as they could sign contracts. And that has all come to a screeching halt, unlike anything I've seen in my 25 years in the business. We have been laying off staff to reduce our overhead, but we still can't meet our obligations. We're behind on our rent payments as well as our utilities, and this has us in a precarious position. We've even had to reduce our advertising budget, which is negatively affecting sales, but there just aren't the funds to continue."

"Sidney, are you saying the chain might fail?"

"I'm sorry. I can't rule out anything right now. StarTrust is now threatening our line of credit, which would probably push us over the edge and into Chapter 11."

One of the other board members spoke up and said, "Don, we can't cut off Two Wyse Guys. That would hurt the bank as much as the store chain."

Don responded, "Jesse, you have a point. We have a team auditing their books to determine their net value. We're hoping to use as much as their assets to cover the loan amounts. We'll have their report in about a week. In the meantime, the chain still owes me personally for the buyout payments according to the terms I have with Sid. I have agreed to suspend those payments for now in an effort to help their cash flow."

Jesse Elkins commented, "That's generous of you Don. We'll just have to wait out the audit report."

Don continued the meeting by saying, "Before we hear from the ELT, I want to report personally that I spoke to Donny Davino Jr. earlier today, and he confirmed that Two Wyse Guys leases were well in arrears. With the exception of the handful of national chain stores, such as Home Depot, Starbucks, Marshall's and others, he was experiencing similar collection problems with all the other tenants in those same malls as foot traffic had fallen to a trickle. He reported the same delinquencies with just about all of his commercial tenants. It was a pervasive situation. And the upshot was that he may default on some of his mortgages."

What was left of the Executive Leadership Team were all sitting in the back, along with Dee Dee, waiting their turn to make their reports and be questioned by the board. Don noticed that Dee Dee looked awful. Her hair was unkempt and her makeup poorly applied. Her face was blotchy and swollen. She had also left the boardroom during Stern's presentation and then returned about 15 minutes later. All of this was out of character for her.

One by one the ELT members gave their dismal report, which reflected and confirmed the problems that Stern had described earlier. StarTrust was feeling the full brunt of the downturn.

When they completed their reports, Don turned to Dee Dee and asked, "Miss Davino, if you know the reason Serena McCormack suddenly resigned, can you share it with us?"

Dee Dee raised her voice and said, "I am the reason she resigned. That bitch has been sexually harassing me for many months and I filed a complaint against her. I just . . ."

Don cut her off, saying, "That's enough. It is inappropriate to share very sensitive information of that type at this venue. And where is Mr. Cogswell? Why isn't he here at this mandatory meeting?"

"Whitney got on a plane yesterday and left for vacation."

Don was incredulous. "What? Can you tell us where he went and when he'll be back? How could he leave town when we're facing a crisis of this magnitude? Couldn't you stop him?"

Dee Dee stood up and at the point of hysteria shouted, "No, I couldn't stop him. He's alone and I don't know where the fuck he went, or when he might be coming back. And you should also know that I'm pregnant and he's the father!" She then grabbed her papers and ran out the door, leaving a room full of totally stunned people behind.

Recovering, Don stood up and announced that he would form a committee to study the bank's dire situation. The team would work quickly to make immediate recommendations for recovery. And he adjourned the meeting.

He then rushed out of the boardroom to comfort his niece. Sadly, she was nowhere to be found.

Chapter 105

Following the tumultuous board meeting, Todd Christopher and Hugo Sanchez each returned to their offices before leaving for the evening. While they were shaken up by all the economic news affecting the bank, they were even more concerned about Dee Dee's surprise announcement. The same thoughts occupied their minds. How can she be sure it was Whit's baby? Is there a DNA test in my future? Were any of the other guys also sleeping with her? They knew nothing good was going to come out of this development.

Shawn, who was devastated by all the news that came from Dee Dee, went home after the meeting and filled Laura in on everything that had transpired. It was obvious that she was again becoming unhinged in the meeting, and so the veracity of her statements was unclear. In discussing it, they felt bad for Serena and sat there trying to piece together the untold story of what really happened between them. Shawn also could not believe that Dee Dee and Whit were sleeping together. She was so loyal, protecting him so carefully, and she was very close to Lucille. Laura agreed that none of this made any sense. They could only wait and see what would emerge.

The next day, Don Davino came back to the bank and visited each of the division executives. Don wanted them to serve on the committee to look into the tenuous position that StarTrust found itself. Don had also invited Jessie Elkins and David Stern, who he engaged to participate. Given the urgency of the situation, the team immediately dove into the review of reports that were available from the various departments. The picture that was forming made the future look even worse than anticipated. And with each succeeding day's reports were progressively bleaker. Don began to seriously wonder if the bank could survive.

Chapter

106

One week later, a team of bank examiners showed up at the bank for an audit. The rumor that spread throughout headquarters was that someone had made an anonymous phone call to the Federal Deposit Insurance Corporation, advising them that StarTrust may be insolvent. They immediately went to Cogswell's office, only to learn from Dee Dee that he was still out of the office and on vacation. While questioning her, one of the auditors let slip a comment about a bank acquisition deal with a New Haven firm. Picking up on this, Dee Dee immediately knew why StarTrust had been selected for this audit.

Within hours, the examination team found enough evidence of a major catastrophe. The lead investigator, Kenneth Carlson asked Dee Dee to call Don Davino and schedule an emergency board meeting for the next day at noon.

In the meantime, Carlson was requesting all reports from the various departments. Perusing them, he took several immediate steps. Every corporate credit card account was cancelled. And any expense checks for executives were frozen. He demanded that Dee Dee track down Whitney, and if she couldn't locate him, his payroll checks would be held up until he returned to the bank. Carlson then called the Fed, confirming that StarTrust Bancorp was insolvent, and requested that a trustee be named to oversee the bank's day-to-day operation until it could be sold.

The next day as he sat in the conference room, which he had taken over as his command center, Dee Dee came in and handed him a large package, saying, "This just came in by messenger for Mr. Cogswell. I though you might want to see it."

Carlson opened the official-looking package. It was a judgment by the Federal District Court for Connecticut Central Bank in New Haven for $12 million against StarTrust Bankcorp and Whitney Cogswell as co-defendants. Since Cogswell had signed the contract without any authorization, alluding that he was qualified to execute such a document, he was considered personally liable.

Later that day Kenneth Carlson called Dee Dee into the conference room and asked her what she knew about the contract with Central Connecticut Bank & Trust. She explained all the details she knew, including her advice to Cogswell to bring the contract to the board for approval, and his apparent failure to do so. She also mentioned the credit card charges by Whitney for activities with Franklin Blauvelt that included lunches, dinners and a large charge to an entertainment company.

Recognizing that Dee Dee had very intimate knowledge of the inner workings of the bank and particularly of Cogswell's activities, he asked her if she would work closely with him to clean up all the loose ends in order to transfer the bank to another institution. It was obvious that procedure and documentation in the executive suite was woefully inadequate, and he realized that there were too many secrets buried here that he would never uncover. Recognizing the opportunity to get her revenge, she agreed with one caveat. She had some serious health issues that required her to take a few weeks off from work. She hadn't had a vacation in over three years, and was totally stressed out. He agreed as long as she would wait one more week before taking her leave.

The directive came down from the Fed that Kenneth Carlson was named the interim CEO of StarTrust. Using his broad powers, he placed the bank in receivership, immediately discharged the entire board of directors and terminated all the remaining members of the Executive Leadership Team.

    The following month all assets of StarTrust Bancorp were transferred to Bank of America with Carlson being named interim CEO of the unit.

Part IV

Epilogue

Scattered Ashes

VI

Angelo & Donny Davino

As the economy began to collapse, Angelo and Donny Davino were totally unprepared to deal with the outcome. Angelo had no choice but to allow much of his equipment to be repossessed. He also began to lay off workers in droves, as maintenance contracts were being cancelled. By slashing his overhead, and ending up with a much smaller staff plus the remaining equipment he owned outright, Angelo managed to survive, servicing his substantially shrunken customer base.

With Two Wyse Guys going bankrupt, Donny Davino found himself in a serious cash crunch. Through Dee Dee's intersession he arranged a meeting with his lawyer, accountant and Kenneth Carlson. Together they worked out a plan for him to restructure most of his mortgages, while selling some of his weaker properties at huge losses. And by making rent concessions with his tenants, most of the remaining retailers were able to hang on and survive the crash.

Donny was able to raise some investment capital by offering shares at well below market prices. It took him several years to recover, but ultimately his empire was rebuilt and it became one of the largest real estate investment trusts in the country.

John Youngman, Tom Mitchell and Bobby Willis

Upon their termination, John Youngman, Tom Mitchell and Bobby Willis each had a very difficult time finding employment. As disgraced bankers, no financial institution would hire them. They each quickly ran through their severance and had to go into their personal savings. Youngman, who had a life insurance license, moved to a Del Webb retirement community outside of Charlotte, NC. As a 55-year old active resident, he befriended everyone and began to offer investment seminars, selling them annuities at huge commissions. Before long, his income grew substantially. But he eventually wore out his welcome as his clients realized that the annuity investments were sub-par. John then packed up and moved to another all-inclusive retirement community and repeated his successful scam.

Bobby Willis, who had a tainted résumé and no marketable skills, could not find a management position of any kind. In desperation after his divorce, he took a sales position with a car dealer. While the income was only modest, he found many dating opportunities with the well-endowed, attractive women that proliferated most auto showrooms.

Tom Mitchell fared the best of the three former ELT executives. Through a former buddy from the Army Reserves, he landed a job with a company that provided auto lease services to credit unions. His commissions and perks provided him with a very comfortable living.

Lucille Cogswell and Don Davino

Lucille Cogswell divorced Whitney for infidelity and abandonment and because of his absence was awarded all the marital assets. She moved to Vero Beach, FL with her parents and became their caretaker as they aged. While her mother was still healthy, she took her to lunch once a week where they shared a bottle of Montipulciano d'Abruzzo. Don Davino tried to stay busy learning golf and playing bocce at the country club in their gated community. But he quickly abandoned those ideas from lack of interest.

Out of boredom, Don began to visit the appliance stores in the area, which were mostly big box outlets of the national chains. He would shake his head at the incompetence of the sales staffs and the pricing gimmicks they offered to unsuspecting customers.

And one day he wandered into a large kitchen and bath showroom, striking up a conversation with the owner. Quickly recognizing Don's in-depth knowledge of appliances, he offered him a position as a consultant to his customer base. Accepting the deal on the spot, Don immediately became a valuable asset advising clients on upgrading their homes and selecting appliances that fit their needs.

As Don became comfortable in his position, he came to relish the opportunity to use his people skills and his acumen of appliances. And more importantly, he no longer had to deal with the stress of running a business and making all those painful decisions that came with managing a retail operation.

Shawn & Laura DiPisa

Laura DiPisa quickly sold her agency to a large advertising conglomerate before the economy completely collapsed. Her contract only required her to stay on for six months. However, her payout was partly predicated on the business that was retained over a three-year period. And since her agency's billing quickly dropped off, the payout diminished rapidly. She wisely banked the upfront payment and all the installments, putting them into their retirement account.

Following Shawn's termination, they decided to sell their beautiful home in Ramsey. The unique five-acre property sold quickly and because they had acquired the land and built the home in the late eighties, they realized a very substantial profit. They also had a very small balance on their mortgage, which left them a large net gain.

They decided to move to Charlotte, NC, where several of the banks that were considered too big to fail were headquartered. They set up a small marketing consulting firm to cater to this large segment of the local economy.

Shawn immediately appreciated the pace of business in this beautiful small city. He put together a portfolio of programs he developed for StarTrust, and quickly got the attention of the marketing executives of the region's major banks. While the banks were interested in restoring their market share, they were also gun-shy and reluctant to dive into extensive promotional campaigns. It took a while to build the business, but as a virtual agency with no overhead, they became profitable within a short period of time. They joined a local country club, and surprisingly found time to enjoy golf together on a regular basis.

Serena McCormack

Immediately upon her resignation, Serena McCormack liquidated her shares of stock in StarTrust BanCorp, sold her fully furnished condo, in Hackensack, and moved to Sarasota, FL. She spent a few months walking the city's beautiful beaches and exploring its downtown cultural attractions, while she unwound from all the pressures of her career at StarTrust.

Finally, getting restless for a new challenge, she started networking and began to volunteer at some of the area's many charity-based organizations. Her credentials were very strong and it wasn't long before she started to get offers for leadership roles at some of these not-for-profits. Serena accepted a role as Executive Director of a large family foundation, where she found the work rewarding and fulfilling.

At a charity symposium held at the University of South Florida campus in Sarasota, Serena met one of the panelists on the forum of the opening session. He was a retired entrepreneur who had sold his business to his employees in an ESOP, while he remained on their board. She was very taken by his decisiveness and convictions as he dominated the discussion during the interactive panel dialog. After the presentation, Serena went up to him and struck up a conversation. And with just a little encouragement from her, he asked her out and began to court her. Maybe, she thought, just maybe she had finally found a real man.

Ed Rothenberg

Shortly after arriving at the US penitentiary in Lewisburg, PA, Ed Rothenberg encountered some of the convicts he had successfully prosecuted when he was with the Attorney General's office in Newark. As word spread that Rothenberg was a former prosecutor, the inmates began to threaten and torment him. Fearing for his life, he had his attorney place calls to colleagues and contacts in state politics, looking for someone who could help move him to a different facility. His lawyer also appealed to the courts pleading for a change in incarceration facilities. All of it was to no avail.

With no chance of outside help coming to his aid, Rothenberg tried to make a deal with gang leaders within the prison. They offered protection if he could come up with regular cash payments, made to a secret bank account. After he agreed to pay $2,000 a month, he set up a payment process with Misti Waters, the only one of his stable of girlfriends that did not come forward during the scandal. She had promised to remain loyal to him and never identified herself or gave an interview to the press. And she had also agreed to leave the country with him during his foiled escape plan.

Rothenberg provided her access to his secret offshore account so she could draw the funds for the extortion payout. But following the first installment, the payments inexplicably stopped coming. Rothenberg could offer the gang leaders no explanation. And a few days later, the former state senator was found bleeding out in a shower, having been stabbed several times. He later died from his wounds.

Misti Waters is now living in a colorful little cottage near the beach on the Cayman Islands. She lives modestly through the funds on deposit in a numbered account at a local bank.

Ben Rusk

By the time Ben Rusk was released from prison, the economy had collapsed, and along with it, StarTrust Bancorp. He served almost four years in the minimum security facility, with no reportable incidents. But he left prison a broken man.

During his incarceration, he planned how he was going to survive once he was free. When he was released, his friend and attorney, Woodrow Horvath lent him some money to help him begin his new life.

Ben rented a modest apartment in Nutley, NJ, and he leased a storefront in an industrial section of Newark. He used the location to open a payday loan and check cashing service. Taking advantage of the poor market conditions and the plight of low-income laborers and factory workers, he thrived cashing their checks, collecting payments for their utility bills and making weekly loans at exorbitant rates to these economically challenged people.

His career had come full circle, and he now relished the opportunity to earn income without the stress. And he also discovered a newfound appreciation for leading a low-profile existence, while making a very substantial income that afforded him a privileged lifestyle.

Whitney Cogswell

When Whitney left his office on that fateful day, he never looked back. At the time when he first realized that his empire might be crumbling, he secretly opened a bank account in San Jose, Costa Rica and quietly transferred small amounts of money that he was embezzling from the bank. Unfortunately for him, there wasn't enough time between his recognition of pending disaster and his unscheduled exit to accumulate very much money in the account.

Arriving in this Central American tourism destination without luggage, he checked into a small hotel and began his search for a permanent residence.

He used his corporate credit card for the one-way flight to Costa Rica, the hotel bill, a complete wardrobe, a new cell phone, and other items. So it was not difficult for Kenneth Carlson's team to track him down. They immediately cancelled his credit card and were attempting to claw back the funds in his bank account. Fortuitously upon arrival, Whit transferred the money to a different account at another bank. Lucille attempted to contact him, but received no response. She sent the divorce papers to his hotel, but he had already moved to a small tourist resort on the beach in Jaco without providing a forwarding address.

It didn't take long for the money to run out, so he was forced to take a job. He made a deal at the resort for free room and board, and became the social director, organizing events for the mostly American tourists. His position also allowed him to romance the single women, along with a few married ones that were guests at the resort. And he made some extra income by giving private tennis lessons to the guests. His drinking and drug usage, which became heavier over time were what ultimately caused his downfall. He got caught selling cocaine to one of the guests at the hotel, was arrested and is still rotting away in a Costa Rican prison.

Dee Dee Davino

Dee Dee had an abortion during her three-week leave and insisted that there be no DNA test. She weaned herself off all her medications and made a vow to get her weight under control.

Accepting the offer from Kenneth Carlson, she became his assistant. They spent the next few months unravelling all the problem issues that Whitney Cogswell and everyone on the entire Executive Leadership Team had created.

Dee Dee then worked closely with Carlson in settling the many lawsuits, restructuring loans and mortgages, cancelling lines of credit, and closing out delinquent accounts.

After the bank was taken over by Bank of America, Carlson became the division president of all the BoA branches in New Jersey.

A short time later, Dee Dee and Kenneth were married and they moved into her Jersey City condo. She had finally found genuine love.

And every once in a while, after a particularly stressful day of crunching numbers and directing the incompetent middle management staff at the various branch locations, Carlson arrived home savoring the opportunity to be Dee Dee's submissive sex slave.

Other books by Michael A. Sisti

Executive Crumple Zone

A gut-wrenching, yet hilarious tale of corporate lunacy describes the clash of cultures between an entrepreneur and the status quo bureaucrats, who thwart his every move. Told as a series of emails, this is a fast paced, must-read novel that you won't put down until it ends.

*Winner- International Book Award 2010

THE FAILURE MYTH

This book is the result of Sisti's experience gained from a forty-year career serving both entrepreneurial and corporate clients, plus his extensive research on why small businesses succeed or fail.

Orsini House, University Park, FL 34201
http://MichaelSisti.com